AF842707

Managing Safety in Complexity

Making 'Working Safely' Possible
Between Systems That Speak Different Codes

— Book One in the *Risk + Safety / Sociology* Series —

Martijn Flinterman

First Edition

www.untersoziologen.com

ISBN/EAN: 978-90-835717-0-6

Foreword

Can you relate to what has happened to me so many times? When things go wrong at work, we often fall back on familiar explanations: human error, non-compliance with safety procedures, or reactive safety culture. These feel intuitive, but I've found they oversimplify the complex reality of how our organisations actually function.

Managing Safety in Complexity offers a different perspective, grounded in Niklas Luhmann's systems theory. In this book, we explore how organisations operate through communication, not just through control, compliance, or consensus. I also describe how systems like law, economy, media, and science each use their own code to understand what 'safety' means.

This is not a book of checklists or slogans, though it examines how those are used. It's written for HSE professionals ready to move beyond root causes and behaviourist tools. Instead of asking, "How can people behave better?" it asks, "How is healthy, safe, and environmentally friendly work even possible between systems that interpret responsibility, risk, and legitimacy in different ways?"

Where popular management books often urge readers to develop emotional intelligence or show heroic leadership, I show how trust, responsibility, and communication depend on structural conditions instead of personality. In doing so, I aim to relieve overburdened professionals and offer more sustainable paths to resilience and safety.

I have written *Managing Safety in Complexity* as a guide for curious, and slightly frustrated HSE professionals. If you're tired of tick-the-box exercises, this is a book for you. Let's disrupt the common assumptions of HSE management!

Martijn Flinterman, Nes, the Netherlands, September 2025

Table of Contents

SYSTEM | UMWELT

In HSE management,
just like anywhere else,
we draw the line between
system and environment[1]
like we draw the line between
us and them.
It's meaning-making.

Us and them
And after all
We're only ordinary men

Roger Waters, 1973

Introducing Luhmann to HSE management

"Niklas Luhmann was the last theoretical giant whose shoulders were worth standing on."
— Norbert Bolz, media theorist[2]

Why bring Luhmann into HSE?
My website Unter Soziologen[3] started as a hobby. I built it after my time at the Graduate School of Delft University of Technology. The aim was to share what I had learned during my deep dive into the sociology of risk. One of the most fascinating and prolific sociologists I encountered was Niklas Luhmann. Luhmann was a systems thinker, and an unusually original one. I saw numerous practical applications for his work, yet noticed that outside of Germany, few people knew of him. That's why I wrote this book.

The paradoxes of HSE practice
If you, like me, work in health, safety and environment (HSE) management, you likely encounter paradoxes regularly. Despite having more rules, reporting systems, and audits than ever before, accidents still occur, sometimes without clear explanations. Even when systems appear to function as intended, unexpected events continue to undermine our carefully engineered defences. The familiar language of 'zero harm', 'root causes', and 'corrective actions' often feels inadequate in a field characterised by complexity, interdependence, and uncertainty.

Enter Niklas Luhmann.

Niklas Luhmann in his study[4]

Who was Niklas Luhmann?
Niklas Luhmann (1927–1998) was a German sociologist who, between 1964 and 1994, developed a systems theory of society. Among his extensive body of work are books that offer a different perspective for understanding organisations and other social systems, and their attempts to manage risk.

Luhmann's life experiences made him sceptical of centralised control, moralising narratives, and simplistic explanations. He grew up under Nazism, hated that regime, but was drafted into World War II. He lost a schoolfriend in battle. After the war, he pursued legal studies and eventually found intellectual refuge in systems theory. He spent time studying with the then famous sociologist Talcott Parsons in the U.S., and over time, broadened his inquiry to include the workings of communication, societal systems, and organisations[5].

Communication over compliance
Luhmann critiqued early system theories, because they assumed coherence where complexity ruled[6]. And that's an important point for us in HSE management. Just as no universal model can explain all social action, no checklist or behavioural metric can capture the full reality of working safely. It can't be understood through idealised systems, like we tend to do so often. Instead, working safely can only be understood through ongoing, recursive communication. We must study how meaning is produced, contested, and adapted in real time. In HSE, this means recognising that safety is never produced by a single cultural change or managerial tool. It emerges at the

intersection of multiple societal systems sucha as law, politics, economy, and science. Each of these generates its own expectations and constraints for how risks are managed. Luhmann critiqued early systems theory[7] because it couldn't explain how systems observe themselves or become blind to their own operations. This is where Luhmann begins, and where modern HSE management must also go.

System, what system?

Deming's systems thinking observed by Luhmann

A lot of systems thinking in organisations is influenced by W. Edwards Deming's System of Profound Knowledge[8] (SoPK). But what might this framework look like from the perspective of Niklas Luhmann's systems theory? Let's look at each of the four SoPK components.

Appreciation for a system

Deming saw systems as networks of interdependent components that work together to accomplish the aim of the system[9]. From Luhmann's perspective, however, 'the system' is not a stable object to be valued. It's a construction that emerges through communicative actions. What is defined as 'the system' depends on how the system observes and differentiates itself from its environment. Systems observe themselves, whether they are psychological systems (individuals) or social systems (networks).

Knowledge about variation

Deming urged organisations to distinguish common-cause variation from special-cause variation to avoid reacting to noise. Luhmann would appreciate this principle, but he would stress that variation in social systems is not just statistical but also interpretive. One subsystem (e.g., operations) may ignore a signal that another subsystem (e.g., HSE) considers critical. 'Error', 'risk', or 'deviation' are not fixed facts, but communicative distinctions with inherent blind spots.

Theory of knowledge

Deming encouraged reflection on how knowledge influences action. Luhmann went further: all knowledge is observational. Every act of knowing involves a distinction; what is seen versus what is excluded. It's not just about what we know, but also about how knowledge is generated, stabilised, and disseminated within the system. Knowledge is thus less about individual cognition and more about organisational communication.

Psychology
Deming underlined the role of psychology in understanding motivation and leadership. For Luhmann, psychology is one of many meaning systems that organisations can use to regulate expectations. But it does not explain the system; it explains how the system assigns meaning to behaviour. According to Luhmann, psychology is not the basis of motivation, but a code for communication about persons.

Conclusion
From Luhmann's perspective, *there is no profound knowledge* in an absolute sense, only different ways of observing, each with their own limitations. Systems reduce the complexity of the environment *by making distinctions*, not by discovering truths. What matters is *how a system observes*, not just *what* it observes.

It's functional differentiation, stupid
Modern society, Luhmann wrote, is composed of distinct social systems such as law, economy, politics, science, and media. Each of these is governed by its own internal logic. Health, safety, and environment are not *things* that exists objectively in the world. Instead, they are *constructed meanings within specific functional systems*, such as the scientific system, the organisational system, or the legal system.

Importantly, in Luhmann's view:
- Each system processes information through its own *binary code of observation: e.g.* truth/untruth in science, legal/illegal in law, profit/loss in the economy.
- Accidents or failures are interpreted differently depending on which system is doing the observing.
- Structures like safety procedures, audits, or human error reports are not objective truths but *communications within particular subsystems*.

People, Systems, and Communication
Sociologist Niklas Luhmann had a different way of looking at organisational systems too. He said that organisations are not made up of people, but of communications. This might sound strange at first. After all, don't people run organisations? Yes, but Luhmann's point is that organisations operate by creating

decisions, rules, and expectations that build on each other over time. These communications form a self-sustaining system.

People are essential. They talk, decide, and act, but they belong to the environment of the system, not the system itself. Think of a theatre play: actors come and go, but the script, roles, and structure of the play continue. In the same way, an organisation continues not because the same people stay forever, but because the system of roles, rules, and decisions keeps going.

This view is very different from approaches like behavioural safety, which focus on individual actions. Luhmann didn't ignore human agency, he simply saw it as part of a larger system of meaning and communication.

Example: The safety report that got ignored

Imagine a worker notices a safety issue on a construction site and writes a report. That's a communication. Whether anything happens next depends not just on the worker, but on how the organisation's communication system handles that report. Does it trigger a meeting? Is there a role responsible for following up? Are decisions based on similar past reports?

If the organisation is set up to respond only to reports that follow a strict format, the real issue might get lost, even if the person acted responsibly. This shows how communication patterns, instead of just human behaviour, influence what gets done.

Dealing with uncertainty

Luhmann also helps us understand that no rulebook can cover everything. Work is local, messy, and often unpredictable. Thinking like Luhmann's and others paved the way for ideas in *resilience engineering*, which says that successful organisations adapt to surprises; they don't try to eliminate uncertainty completely.

Formal procedures help, but they can also limit flexibility. More rules don't always mean more safety. Sometimes, they leave less room for people to reflect, speak up, or adjust when conditions change.

Luhmann saw that modern organisations juggle many goals at once: profit, legal compliance, safety, health, and more. No single goal rules over the others. This complexity and pluralism are what *resilience* is all about: being able to adapt instead of just control.

A different way of looking

Rather than saying we need tighter control, Luhmann suggests to see the situation differently. He asks us to think of *roles, rules, and norms as tools for managing complexity*, instead of as fixed truths. This doesn't mean we stop making judgments. It means we judge differently, and ask: "What *function* does this rule serve?" or "What kind of *communication* does this structure support or block?"

In the end, Luhmann's work reminds us that to understand organisations, we need to look not just at what people do, but at *how meaning and decisions are made and remade over time*.

How to read this book

This book aims to make Luhmann's ideas accessible and relevant for the practice of managing health, safety, and environment. His work reveals the blind spots in our current assumptions and offers new perspectives for reflection, design, and asking better questions. This is a book for practitioners who want to work *with* complexity, rather than *against* it. I invite you to go on this journey with me.

I definitely don't intend this book as a manual for HSE management. I don't offer quick fixes, step-by-step checklists, or generic best practices. Rather, I invite you into a different way of thinking, one informed by Niklas Luhmann's systems theory and the complexity of real organisational life. If you are looking for clear answers, you may find instead a set of better questions.

You can read this book in more than one way:

a. Cover to cover (the *immersive* route)

If you are new to Luhmann or want to fully understand how systems theory can reframe HSE management, start at the beginning and move chapter by chapter. The book builds progressively, from basic distinctions like risk and safety, toward more abstract ideas like second-order observation and symbolic generalisation. I designed each chapter to stand on its own (hence there is some repetition in terms), but each also connects with what comes before and after.

b. By topic or question (the *reflective* route)

You don't need to read this book in a straight line, though. You can think of it as an *atlas of safety paradoxes*. Each chapter tackles a different tension, challenge, or blind spot in managing safety in complex organisations. At the start of each chapter, you'll find *keywords* that point to its theme. Use these as signposts. If you're wrestling with a specific problem, start with the chapters that resonate most:

When learning goes wrong or blame dominates:
- Chapter 1 – *When learning goes off script*.

Making sense of systems and communication:
- Chapter 2 – *How systems patch meaning into safety*;
- Chapter 3 – *Understanding operationally closed systems*.

Struggling with risk communication:
- Chapter 4 – *Understanding the system's hearing problem*;
- Chapter 5 – *Entertain us: The ritual life of risk*.

Curious about audits, procedures, and legitimacy:
- Chapter 6 – *Form before function: Procedural safety*.

Dealing with trust, power, and messy management systems:
- Chapter 7 – *Power, trust, and HSE management systems*.

Wanting to understand rule-breaking and *useful illegality*:
- Chapter 8 – *Rule-Breaking as a system function?*

Wondering how morality creeps into safety debates:
- Chapter 9 – *Morality as a safety strategy?!*

Frustrated with goals that legitimise but don't guide:
- Chapter 10 – *How goals legitimise but rarely guide action*.

Exploring leadership under uncertainty:
- Chapter 11 – *Leadership in structurally opaque systems*.

Asking about the limits of control, and safety creating its own risks:
- Chapter 12 – *How safety constructs its own risks*;
- Chapter 13 – *Designing for not-knowing*.

Looking for ways to navigate paradoxes and complexity head-on:
- Chapter 14 – *Managing complexity without illusion*.

Wanting a *big picture* Luhmannian take on HSE:
- Chapter 15 – *Luhmann's HSE Management*.

Each chapter blends three elements:
- Real-world examples of how safety plays out in practice;
- Theoretical perspectives to reframe the challenge;
- Conceptual tools to help you think and act differently.

Choose your own entry point. Follow the thread of your current challenge, or wander through the atlas to see how the themes connect.

c. As a companion for dialogue (the *conversational* route)
This book isn't meant to be read in isolation. Many of the ideas come alive in dialogue, with colleagues, teams, students, or during reflection after incidents. Like I did myself.

You can use the book as a thinking partner:
- Bring a chapter into a team debrief.
- Compare it with existing safety models you use.
- Use the concepts to challenge assumptions in your organisation.

Think of this as a systems perspective book, not as a rulebook.

Some tips for reading:
- Pause often. Many ideas may feel counterintuitive or disruptive. That's intentional.
- Watch for distinctions. Luhmann's theory operates through distinctions: safe/unsafe, observed/unobserved, formal/informal. Pay attention to how they are drawn, and what they exclude.
- Use the margins to annotate, question, and argue. The book is a conversation starter. Luhmann has many followers, professors and students, who treat his theories not as an orthodoxy, but as a kaleidoscope that shows new images all the time.

A note on language
Luhmann's writing can be dense and abstract. One of the reasons for that, is that Luhmann produced his books by means of his filing cabinet (called '*Zettelkasten*'). All material and references that seemed relevant were collected in it, to be later used in numbered chapters without a title under one subject. Because of using this method, there's a lot of repetition in Luhmann's writing too. I've tried to make his ideas accessible without oversimplifying. Occasionally, I quote him directly, when the precision of his wording matters. But mostly, I translate his theory into practice.
In short: Read this book as a guide for thinking, instead of control. Safety is not something we achieve and then protect. It's something we construct, lose, and reconstruct, over and over, through communication.
If you finish this book more uncertain than when you began, but are asking sharper questions; then I'm happy: it has done its job.

Chapter 1 – When learning goes off script

Keywords: Regret, Blame, Systemic Distortion

"No realli! She was Karving her initials øn the møøse with the sharpened end of an interspace tøøthbrush given her by Svenge - her brother-in-law - an Oslo dentist and star of many Norwegian møvies: 'The Høt Hands of an Oslo Dentist', 'Fillings of Passion', 'The Huge Mølars of Horst Nordfink'..."

We apologise for the fault in the subtitles. Those responsible have been sacked[10]*.*

"Mynd you, møøse bites Kan be pretty nasti..."

We apologise again for the fault in the subtitles. Those responsible for sacking the people who have just been sacked, have been sacked.

(...) *The directors of the firm hired to continue the credits after the other people had been sacked, wish it to be known that they have just been sacked. The credits have been completed in an entirely different style at great expense and at the last minute.*

— Monty Python and the Holy Grail opening credits[11]

Don't you love Monty Python's humour? I do. Great humour disrupts expectations. We don't expect the subtitles to be open about personnel decisions at the film company. But humour often contains a grain of truth as well. And just as in this Monty Python storyline, organisations often use blame and rewrite narratives when things go wrong. Responsibility becomes performative, and communication resets itself without learning.

Regret as a system distorter

"If later developments not only increase the estimated costs but also lead to regretting the decision, what possible responses are available? The most harmless is probably: a ritual sacrifice." - Luhmann[12]

Luhmann wrote that, in hindsight, even low-probability risks somehow seem inevitable. As soon as damage occurs, the uncertainty and hope that accompanied the original decision disappear. In its place come regret, pressure, and a collective urge to rethink both past stories and future processes. Luhmann understood this as a systemic tension: organisations need stable expectations, but society demands accountability afterward[13].

> *"Terrible accident. Gets a lot of media exposure. We could just sack the operator. It would save us a lot of money that would go into re-engineering the human-machine interface."*
>
> Manager observed during fieldwork

We may find this quote cynical. I was shocked when I heard it. At the same time, it shows that organisations tend to respond to systemic shortcomings with individual blame. From Luhmann's perspective, this is a functional mechanism. It's an attempt to restore trust and legitimacy to the system by personalising the cause. By turning a complex interaction of technology, design, and communication into a question of "who failed", the organisation simplifies its environment and avoids costly self-observation. Luhmann called this the *management of decision premises*. It happens when organisations don't focus on structural problems but on visible, symbolically satisfying actions instead. The system protects itself by punishing deviations, not by learning from complexity.

Firing the operator is not (only) retaliation. It's a communication signal, saying to regulators, investors, and the public: "We acted." But what contributes to the risk (the flawed interface, the normalisation of deviant behaviour, and the absence of feedback loops) remains untouched.

I don't use the quote to shock you like I was myself at the time, but to ask some questions:
- What does this decision communicate?
- What complexity does it avoid?
- What would be needed to make the system observe itself?

When something goes wrong, organisations:
- Reinterpret decisions with new causal stories,
- Launch investigations to restore order,
- Often impose symbolic punishments by blaming individuals, including those who did nothing wrong.

These rituals help the organisation maintain continuity without making deep changes. As Luhmann noted, systems often prefer to re-legitimise their existing path rather than take the risk of innovation.

The paradox of learning from exceptions
"*In serious cases, commissions are set up to restore order in what had to be experienced as chance*." – Luhmann[14]

Learning from exceptions may seem sensible, but it often distorts the perception of risk, Luhmann wrote. When a disaster threatens to become too big to handle, decision-making slows under the weight of defensive bureaucracy. When this happens, opportunity gives way to risk aversion. Organisations then create new procedures in order to prevent yesterday's surprise, and in the hope of also preventing tomorrow's challenge. Luhmann observed that this leads to:
- Excessively long approval chains,
- Burdensome documentation,
- Paralysis in the face of rare threats.

Ironically, the intention to prevent failure in this way can lead to inaction.

Rewriting the past to save the present
"*Ongoing irritation from cases where something went wrong gradually transforms into programmed caution. (...) The organisation's risk aversion becomes a danger to those affected in its environment*." - Luhmann[15]

When organisations take risks, they do so under uncertainty. But when something goes wrong, the wisdom comes in hindsight: "We should have seen it coming," you hear. Even if the decision was reasonable, the outcomes change perceptions.

What seemed like a smart choice becomes a reckless gamble. Organisations not only change their policies. They rewrite the past as well. They appoint committees, attribute blame, and sometimes sacrifice leaders to restore public trust. But learning is difficult when the real incentive is to protect the existing narrative.

After a minor traffic accident at a recently renovated company entrance, a senior manager reacts strongly and urges the safety professional to immediately revise the layout: "The design is faulty! Just reverse the entrance and exit like it was beforehand; that will definitely help!". The manager bases his request on urgency, optics, and liability. But the safety professional investigates the incident, determines that it was due to a failure to see because of high shrubbery, and therefore does not accept the manager's urging to change the entrance. Instead, the safety professional treats it as a one-time deviation and recommends regular trimming of shrubbery instead of a costly redesign.
No further incidents occur. Subsequent reviews confirm that the new entrance design meets all safety and traffic standards, and that the manager's initial response was premature. The professional's decision not to accept the manager's immediate recommendation prevents unnecessary changes and ensures a solid and safe design.

Conclusion:
In this case, *not* accepting a reactive correction was the most responsible act. It illustrates that in organisational systems, acceptance is a judgment about what distinctions matter. By avoiding a hasty rewrite of history, the safety professional upheld systemic integrity. As Luhmann reminds us, communication is not the transmission of truth, but selection and interpretation. And sometimes, the best action is a well-reasoned pause.

Bad cases make bad laws

To avoid being trapped in this cycle of *post-decision regret*, we rather could:

- Distinguish between singular tragedies and broader patterns,
- Avoid overgeneralising from emotional shocks,
- Protect the decision-making framework, even under scrutiny.

This is especially urgent in public-facing systems, where the clash between external outrage and internal logic is frequent. In the aftermath of accidents, governance requires self-restraint instead of action for appearance's sake. For this reason, Luhmann warned: "bad cases make bad laws".

Between regret and routine

From reactive blaming to systemic understanding

In this chapter we saw how systems often respond to accidents with remedial stories rather than with real learning. After a failure, they ask not just: "What went wrong?", but also: "Who did something wrong?" This helps to restore order but doesn't necessarily provide comprehension. The danger of this is not only that we regret the decision, but also that we are myopic after the decision. We revise the past to defend the present. Now imagine that we looked not only at the failure, but also at the functions of what happened? In HSE management it's tempting to focus on what breaks, but most systems don't fail most of the time. This fact is more interesting than it seems. The ordinary, the unremarkable, the *nothing happened today* is in fact an improbable systemic achievement.

Where this first chapter explored the distortions of hindsight after some exceptional event, Chapter 2 focuses on foresight. What do we miss when we assume that safety is simply the absence of failure? Let's focus our attention there, on the informal signals, and the quiet acts of coordination. Let's, in other words, look how people fix the hole where the rain gets in, before it turns into a flood we can no longer ignore.

Chapter 2 – How systems patch meaning into safety

Keywords: Systems Theory, Organisational Communication, Proactive Safety

I'm fixing a hole where the rain gets in
And stops my mind from wandering
Where it will go
Fixing a Hole (Beatles)
Paul McCartney, 1967

What makes work safe?
What makes work safe? Rules, training, and good intentions help, but safety often lives in mundane places: the unscheduled chat, the half-glanced signal, and the familiar interaction between colleagues in routine complexity.

An oil refinery[16]

The morning that went right

It's 6:35 AM at a chemical processing plant on the edge of town. The early shift is just beginning. As always, the operators run through the morning startup routine. The checklist gets filled out, mostly from memory. A quick chat at the coffee machine seems to cover more than a formal handover could. One technician notices a faint buzzing sound coming from a pump. He doesn't report it, but he walks a bit slower past that area during his next round.

A new control room operator, still finding her rhythm, accidentally clicks the wrong tab on her screen. The supervisor, glancing over her shoulder while pouring coffee, casually points it out. She nods, embarrassed, and corrects it without saying a word. No incident report is written. No near miss is logged. It's just another morning.
Half an hour later, a maintenance crew improvises a fix using a worn-out part they've learned to trust from experience; something that isn't in the manual but *works*.
Outside, a delivery truck arrives two hours early. No one was expecting it, but a forklift driver happens to be passing by. He calls someone from logistics, who reroutes another vehicle to make space. Again: there's no disruption, no escalation, and no record.

By 10:00 AM, production is stable. No one notices how many tiny adjustments, informal signals, and silent corrections have occurred to make the shift feel... uneventful.

This is what normal looks like. But look again, and you'll see something strange: that smooth operation, the "nothing went wrong" of the day, depended on countless moving parts lining up, most of them invisible, improvised, or undocumented.

Why did the technician linger by that pump? Why did the supervisor notice the screen click? How did the logistics team adapt on the fly? And how did it all seem so routine? That's the puzzle I explore in this chapter. Because when we treat normal functioning as the baseline, we miss the deeper question: *How is this improbable normal even possible?*

Luhmann's perspective: *The improbable normal*
If you have bought this book, you are probably interested enough in HSE management to be familiar with the question: "Should we study accidents (essentially: *unsafety*), or should we study normal work?" It was Professor Erik Hollnagel who made famous the distinction between Safety-I and Safety-II[17]: the tension between focusing on what goes wrong versus what usually goes right. Other ways to pose similar questions have been developed, and we will look into them in chapter 15. Let's take this question to Luhmann: Is safety the absence of failure or the presence of resilient functioning?

As Niklas Luhmann sketched his general theory of social systems from 1964 onwards[18], he distinguished these two approaches:
- We can assume an order as given and problematise its defects, or
- We can consider the normal as unlikely.

Applied to safety, we have these two types of theory:
1. *Accident theory* assumes a normative or ideal order as the baseline (e.g. health and safety) and focuses on identifying and analysing deviations from this norm (e.g. disease, accidents). The assumption is that the system is generally safe or functional, and the goal is to understand why accidents or unsafe conditions occur. A classic example Luhmann notes is the medical approach to health and illness, where the emphasis is on diagnosing and curing diseases. Another example is the sociological study of some kind of social problem which concentrates on deviant behaviours. Economic theories like Keynes's also fit here, Luhmann writes, as they begin with issues such as economic crises and unemployment. We see this perspective used a lot in HSE management. It assumes an ideal state: a functional, safe, and orderly one, and deviations from this norm are the primary concern. It's Hollnagel's Safety-I avant-la-lettre.

2. The *improbable normal theory* starts from the premise that the normal, reliable, safe functioning of systems is unlikely and requires explanation. This approach involves a more abstract and counterfactual mode of thinking (see box below), questioning how safety and order are maintained despite inherent uncertainties and potential for disorder. The theory might ask, "How is working safely even possible at all?" and investigate the conditions and mechanisms that allow for consistent safe operations. This view asks us to change our

understanding of normalcy from something guaranteed to something fragile, constantly recreated through communication. This helps us to explore how regular, safe functioning emerges from a fundamentally unstable or unsafe baseline. Something for that David Woods and Richard Cook, in 2017, coined the term SNAFU: "System Normal: All Fouled Up"[19].

Now, why did Luhmann choose to pursue this second type of theory? Because he saw that reductionist models can't fully explain the complexity of systems: The complexity inherent in social, technical, biological and ecological life, makes it necessary to see systems as fluid and evolving constructs instead of static entities.

Counterfactual Thinking: Useful distinction or misleading trap?

Counterfactuals are common in HSE management:

If only the operator had stopped the job...

If only the inspection had flagged this...

If only the warning light had worked...

These counterfactuals imagine better outcomes and often express regret, blame, or resolve. But they can become traps: oversimplifying causes, masking system complexity, and creating the illusion that failure was obvious but ignored. Such thinking distorts learning[20]. Safety researcher Johan Bergström[21] shows how it narrows explanations. Counterfactuals:

- Focus on simple fixes (e.g., more training),
- Blend emotion with analysis,
- Reduce systemic issues to individual errors,
- Confirm biases instead of challenging them,
- Offer closure instead of curiosity.

Luhmann's counterfactual: A broader view

Unlike traditional counterfactuals, Niklas Luhmann asks:

- *What had to be true for this to seem normal, until it wasn't?*
- *What routines or assumptions hid this risk?*
- *What alternatives were ignored to preserve a sense of order?*

His approach doesn't look at failure but at the conditions of normality. It reveals how systems stabilise themselves through simplifications and blind spots, so that outcomes appear inevitable, until they suddenly aren't.

As safety professionals, we can re-purpose counterfactuals:

- From *"what went wrong?"* → *"how did this become acceptable?"*
- From *"who failed?"* → *"what influenced our expectations?"*
- From *"how do we stop this?"* → *"what does this say about how we frame reality?"*

In short: pair emotional hindsight with systemic foresight.

The loop of interdependence

Luhmann wrote that each participant in a social system acts based on the expected actions of subjects such as colleagues, supervisors, or inspectors. Objects such as procedures, checklists, appliances, tools, or indicators also carry expectations and communicate meaning. This creates a loop of interdependence that no person can resolve independently through individual actions or comprehension influenced by socialisation. Resolving the loop of interdependence is done through continuously addressing, responding, and adjusting to the messages from others (subjects and objects) within the system.

Systems justify their actions through patterns of communication such as routine messages, decisions, reports that assign meaning and responsibility. In the context of HSE, the loop of interdependence necessitates ongoing vigilance and proactive communication among all system participants. HSE is not solely the responsibility of individual actions, but a collective outcome derived from the interaction of all subjects and objects involved. It's about systemic vulnerabilities, risk-laden environments, and conditions prone to failure or harm. Therefore, I suggest we think of HSE management not as a wall that keeps danger out, but as a tent held up by many shifting poles. If one moves, the whole thing readjusts. It stays up not by rigidity, but by flexible, ongoing coordination.

Engaging with complexity

The improbable normality of social systems pertains to their ability to manage and mitigate the complexities of their environments through communication strategies. Systems engage with complexity, break it down, and reconstitute it in ways that line up with their ongoing processes and goals. This involves a constant balancing act between external pressures and internal capacities. Communication serves as the mechanism for negotiating these pressures and enabling the system to function effectively. Engaging with complexity in HSE means understanding that hazards are not static but evolve as conditions change. Effective HSE management systems, therefore, must adapt their communication and control measures dynamically to address emerging risks and ensure resilience against potential failures.

Systemic dynamics
Systems are driven by the need to manage interrelations among numerous elements effectively. The meaning and relevance of actions are derived not just from immediate contexts but from their roles within these dynamic relational structures. We therefore must not focus on individual actions, but on dynamics within the system. We need to understand actions as part of an interconnected system. We don't primarily focus on preventing individual failures, but on enhancing the system's ability to function safely under a variety of conditions.

From "What is this system?" to "How do we currently observe this system?"
The improbable normality of social (or socio-technical) systems is not just a different way to *describe* systems, but a different way to *know* and *observe* them too. It challenges how we come to understand social/socio-technical phenomena like organisations, HSE and risk. We take the focus from *what* a system is (a network of elements) to *how* a system observes, processes, and maintains itself.

Luhmann warned that describing organisations like machines that can be inspected and optimised leads to an illusion of control and clarity. Systems, especially social (or socio-technical) ones, are far from neatly bounded machines. They're dynamic, evolving, and full of internal contradictions. Instead of seeing a system as a stable container, Luhmann sees it as a pattern of communication that is constantly reproducing itself. Order isn't something a system has, but something it does. Each day, through routines, expectations, distinctions, feedback, and decisions, the system recreates its own version of order. And this is never complete or final, because it must continuously respond to internal tensions and external complexity. While traditional safety theory starts with the assumption that order is the norm and failure the deviation, order rather is improbable, always at risk of collapse, and therefore in need of explanation.

Seeing safety as a systemic achievement
Accidents therefore are not the exception, but part of the system's operation. And communication is the medium in which safety is achieved or lost. Daily coordination, expectations, and routines form fragile, provisional 'safety zones'. Systems reduce complexity but do this always incompletely. Therefore, safety is not found in eliminating error, but in adapting and anticipating variability. Knowing the actual nature of real work leads to the

creation of more resilient systems that are able to anticipate and respond to inevitable change[22].

From Luhmann's point of view, HSE management isn't about making the system healthy, safe, and environmentally friendly, but about the improbable possibility that healthy, safe, and environmentally performance can be maintained:
- No system is naturally safe (healthy etc).
- Failure is not an anomaly but a shadow of normal functioning.
- Safety is not a state to reach, but a condition to keep regenerating.

So, the next time someone asks: "Is safety the absence of accidents or the presence of resilience?" ... you might answer: "It's neither. Safety is the improbable outcome of continuous communication, maintained only by the recursive, self-observing work of the system!" And then ask back: "How is safety currently made visible, and what does that visibility exclude?"

If safety is a systemic achievement, then who decides what counts as safe? And how do systems make that distinction?

The same cable, two different outcomes
A technician trips over a loose cable. The report logs it as a minor incident: "no injury". The facilities team shrugs: the line supervisor marks it as closed. A week later, someone else trips over the same cable. This time there's a broken wrist and a formal investigation. Same cable, same environment. So why did the first one barely register? Because what counts as a safety issue depends on how the system sees it.
That might sound cynical, but it's not. It's a structural reality. As Luhmann argued, systems don't respond to the world directly. They respond to what makes sense within their own way of seeing. And they see by drawing distinctions: between safe/unsafe, human error/system failure, normal/deviant. Each distinction brings something into view, and leaves something else out.

Systems create meaning through distinctions and blind spots

Luhmann argued, following mathematician George Spencer Brown's *Laws of Form*, that every distinction creates a form: what is marked (seen) and what is unmarked (ignored). To say something is 'safe' is to implicitly define what is 'unsafe'. Meaning always involves making such distinctions, and with each one, we risk overlooking something else. Each form reveals something while concealing something else. This invisibility is built into the act of selection. For instance, when an incident is categorised as 'human error', the system has made a distinction:

- Marked space: Human error is visible, discussable, addressable.
- Unmarked space: System design, management decisions, and environmental context might be ignored unless someone intentionally brings them into view.

> **Example: The safe factory floor**
>
> Imagine a factory where a manager says, "This area is safe for workers. The guardrails are in place, noise levels are within legal limits, and the workers are trained and follow procedures." In this framing, 'safe' refers to compliance with known rules and visible hazards. But by marking certain things as 'safe', other things automatically become unmarked and unseen:
>
> - Is the pace of work forcing workers to take shortcuts?
> - Are people too fatigued to follow procedures properly?
> - Are maintenance issues going unreported because of pressure to keep machines running?
>
> These unmarked spaces (staffing levels, production pressure, emotional stress) may be left out of the conversation because they're not part of how 'safety' is currently defined. They become blind spots unless someone actively changes the frame. So, the distinction 'safe/unsafe' is a constructed filter. It determines what the organisation sees, discusses, and acts on.

Why This Matters

Luhmann, building on Spencer Brown, would say: every time a system makes a distinction, like 'safe vs unsafe', it also creates a boundary of what it's not seeing. That's the blind spot. This is why he promotes second-order observation:

Not just: What are we calling safe? But: how did we come to define it that way? And what might we be missing as a result? Every time we choose a distinction, we create a blind spot. This is why Luhmann encourages second-order observation. Not just seeing *what* we see, but *how* we see. It's not just about what the organisation pays attention to, but how it decides what's worth paying attention to in the first place.

How much complexity can categorisation handle?
Every organisation functions by observing and communicating differences. But what gets noticed depends on the observer and their distinctions. A judge, a scientist, and a politician can look at the same situation and reach entirely different conclusions:
- A judge considers whether the action fits within a legal framework.
- A scientist evaluates whether a statement is true.
- A politician weighs public perception and strategic consequences.

In HSE management, we do the same. We apply distinctions to risk, safety, health, and environment. For instance, we separate internal risks from decisions or actions from external dangers like weather or supply chain disruption. These distinctions appear in tools like risk matrices or audit categories. But without reflection, they can oversimplify complex realities.

What do you mean when you say "Safe"?

The Safe or Not Safe Game

'Safety' feels like common sense, until you need to define it. Then the comfortable binary of safe/unsafe of a children's game[23] dissolves into opinions, assumptions, and sometimes even marketing.

Consider these, admittedly playfully chosen, online examples:

- Microwave vein closure

"Yes, it's safe... medically approved by registered consultants."
Translation: Microwaves are scary, unless someone in a white coat uses them.

- Mouth taping at night to sleep better

"Yes, it's safe if you do it right."
Translation: Suffocation is possible, because *I'm* afraid to do it wrong!

- Travelling in the Middle East

"Yes, it's safe... but avoid volatile areas."
Translation: Safety by exception.

- Safari excursions

"Yes, it's safe, because your guide has been dodging elephants since birth."
Translation: Somehow comforting?

These examples reveal that 'safety' is not a universal fact, but an observer-dependent construction. Each observer has different reference groups and is socialised *with* or *against* the common opinion of a specific risk.

When categories hide more than they reveal
Categorisation is meant to reduce complexity. But sometimes it reduces the wrong things. A dropdown list in an incident administration module offers 'operator error', but not 'invisible user interface'. Incident reports claim 'technical failure' or 'human error' but leave out 'design mismatch' or 'ambiguous affordance'. Take the next case, for example.

Den Uyl Bridge, the Netherlands[24]

Case example – A bridge fatality
A female cyclist in Zaandam, the Netherlands, died when a bridge opened beneath her. Procedurally, everything functioned as designed: signals sounded, cameras worked, the bridge moved. But the operation had changed:

- From local control to remote monitoring.
- From a single bridge to multiple structures per operator.
- From direct visibility to small video feeds on a cluttered screen.

The cyclist, in hindsight, is thought to have misunderstood the markings. She stood, fatally, on the opening section. The system labelled this as 'human error'. But that hid:

- The ergonomics of the interface.
- The limits of attention across multiple assets.
- The user's incomplete visibility of danger.

The system's technical definition of "safe" excluded the human experience.

Reintroducing distinctions to see the unseen

From Luhmann's perspective, the Den Uyl Bridge case reveals how systems close around pre-defined distinctions. The logic of the technical system (function/failure) overruled the reality of the human user. To overcome this, organisations must become reflexive:

- What distinctions do our safety systems make visible?
- And what realities do they keep invisible?

Seeing more with systemic tools like FRAM and CAST

Systemic methods like FRAM (Functional Resonance Analysis Method, Hollnagel[25]) and CAST (Causal Analysis based on STAMP, Leveson[26]) could help us:

- Map complex, interacting factors.
- Avoid blame.
- Surface deeper system patterns.

Both methods offer a way to move beyond linear causality and simple failure models.

- FRAM recognises that variability in daily performance is normal and that both success and failure can arise from the same functional dynamics. Rather than identifying root causes, FRAM maps how functions vary and interact. It shows how systemic resonance rather than isolated failures can lead to unexpected outcomes.
- CAST, which builds on STAMP (Systems-Theoretic Accident Model and Processes), reframes safety as a control problem rather than a reliability problem. CAST encourages us to analyse accidents by examining safety constraints, control structures, feedback loops, and communication at all levels of the system, including management and policy. It helps to discover why safety constraints failed, rather than who failed to enforce them.

These tools help change our focus from blaming individuals to examining how the system enables or constrains actions. This helps to avoid hindsight bias and promotes meaningful learning. These methods broaden what the system can observe. However, they require time and curiosity, which many organisations undervalue.

What is safety in your system?

So, to improve safety, reflect on your system's internal logic:

- How are risk categories selected?
- What assumptions do they rely on?
- What complexity is filtered out?

Of course this does not mean we need to discard structures, like the incident administration system. But we must examine how our tools construct what we take to be real: WGSMGS: What Gets Seen, Might Get Solved. Every categorisation model makes something visible, and something invisible. Now, why do social systems make these kinds of selections? To reduce complexity, as we discussed before and will now see in detail.

Chapter 3 - Understanding operationally closed systems

Keywords: Complexity Reduction, Operational Closure, Systemic Adaptation

Telephone Line,
Give me some time,
I'm living in twilight
Telephone Line (Electric Light Orchestra)
Jeff Lynne, 1976

Why complexity matters so much
HSE management in our organisations seems often tasked with managing ever-growing complexity. But what does that complexity actually consist of, and how do social systems handle it[27]?

As the number of system elements increases, the number of possible relationships between them increases exponentially. The environment always contains more possibilities, events, and disturbances than any system can absorb. This is what Luhmann defined as *complexity*, it's not merely complicated, but it's *the impossibility of total connectivity*[28].

To function at all, a system must reduce this overwhelming complexity into something manageable. It does this by making selections: deciding what counts, what doesn't, what fits into the frame of relevance, and what gets ignored. Complexity reduction is not optional; it's a *precondition* for system formation and continued operation.

Managing safety in a large manufacturing plant
Imagine an HSE team responsible for overseeing safety in a plant with:

- 300 employees,
- Dozens of machines and processes,
- Multiple contractors,
- Unstable production schedules,
- Regulatory audits, and
- Environmental hazards (chemicals, noise, heat)

At any moment, hundreds of things could go wrong, from a small slip on a wet floor to a catastrophic machine failure. And there are countless inputs flowing into the system: sensor alerts, safety observations, near-miss reports, inspection data, regulatory updates, emails, incident investigations, worker complaints, and more.

The HSE system can't pay attention to everything at once. It's structurally impossible to monitor every interaction between people, machines, tasks, and external factors. It's also impossible to follow up on every safety report with the same depth, and to investigate every possible cause of every incident. Even keeping every risk assessment fully up to date in real time is impossible. There are too many elements, too many possible relationships, and not enough capacity; this is what Luhmann calls complexity.
To remain functional, the HSE system must filter metrics. E.g. it focuses on lost-time injuries, instead on near-misses and fatigue. It prioritises those reports that fit into predefined categories (e.g. "PPE violation"). It uses standard forms that frame incidents in terms of behaviour or compliance. And it allocates resources to the most visible or auditable risks. These are necessary reductions of complexity. But they have a cost.

By filtering complexity, the cumulative impact of production pressure on 'safe behaviour' becomes invisible. So do subtle patterns of near misses that don't fit the report template. Workers might feel moral or emotional concerns that they don't express in formal reports. And, risks that emerge between categories, such as simultaneous maintenance and production get implicitly filtered as well.

How systems reduce complexity
Luhmann described two mechanisms by which social systems reduce complexity:
- By generalisation; the system responds to diverse events with a common rule or routine. Even when situations differ, they are treated as equivalent for the sake of manageability.
- By stepwise selectivity; change is not continuous, but occurs in leaps, such as crises, reforms, and changes after external audits. These stepwise changes allow subsystems to remain loosely coupled. Just like your brain keeps working when your stomach hurts, systems buffer local disruptions without total collapse.

Importantly, Luhmann stressed[29] that *complexity is not the opposite of simplicity*. Simplicity isn't what's left over once you manage complexity; it's a different kind of structure altogether. In reality, what we often deal with is *complex complexity;* systems so dense that even their ways of simplifying become complex.

Complexity is not just out there; it's in the system too
When systems begin to observe themselves, they become *hypercomplex*. Think of a planner inside an organisation who must consider not only the plan, but how others perceive that plan, and how that perception shapes behaviour. The result: recursive loops of "plans about plans," "reviews of reviews," "safety protocols about safety protocols."

This is a structural feature of self-referential systems. As Luhmann wrote, systems are operationally closed: they can't connect to everything around them or even fully translate other systems. Instead, each system constructs its own reality using its own distinctions. What counts as 'risk', 'safety', or 'compliance' depends on internal coding, instead on objective facts from the environment.

From managing complexity to understanding closure
Traditional HSE thinking often stresses that we should manage complexity through control: more procedures, tighter compliance, and clearer metrics. But this approach underestimates how systems actually operate.

Luhmann invites us to move from managing complexity to understanding the conditions under which systems can function at all. This means accepting that:

- Systems can't fully represent their environment;
- Communication is selective and influenced by internal distinctions;
- Different systems (law, politics, economy, operations, media) speak in different codes and can't be fully translated into one another.

Paradoxically, freedom emerges from this closure. Because systems can't control each other, they must treat one another's autonomy as a structural reality. They must *coordinate instead of command*. They communicate through signals instead of instructions. This is the real terrain of modern safety management.

From goals to survival
In a complex system, the idea that organisations pursue fixed goals becomes untenable. Goal setting like Zero Harm may describe aspiration, but it doesn't explain how systems *actually* function under pressure. As Luhmann observed[30], many organisational actions can't be fully explained by goals; they are heavily influenced by routines, social expectations, and the need to appear rational to others.

Two models attempt to explain this:

- The *goal model* assumes a stable environment where actions are planned and optimised.
- The *survival model* suggests systems must constantly adapt to unpredictable conditions to maintain continuity.

But Luhmann writes[31] that even the survival model is *undercomplex* if it doesn't specify *what* needs to survive. Continuity becomes a tautology if we don't examine how systems selectively stabilise themselves: what roles, what expectations, what structures get preserved? Luhmann proposes we treat goals not as drivers, but as *retrospective justifications for already selected structures*. Survival, meanwhile, is not a guarantee but *a continual process of self-stabilisation under uncertainty*. Let's take this theory into the field, with a fictionalised case study.

When safety becomes optional

NordTek is an engineering firm specialising in offshore wind turbine maintenance. It's known for its commitment to safety and sustainability, and has won awards for its Health, Safety and Environment (HSE) compliance. Based on national labour laws and international HSE standards, company policies required technicians working at height to take a mandatory 30-minute rest every 2 hours, have all safety harnesses checked by three people before each climb, record all near misses and submit them for review daily. In practice, during tight project deadlines, especially as weather windows approached, team leaders routinely told technicians: "Skip the third check, we just did one an hour ago." "Keep going for another half hour and rest after the job is done." "Don't record that misstep, it will result in an incident review, and we will lose a day." These instructions were never written down. Everyone knew the rules, and everyone knew when and why they should be broken. Technicians who refused to be 'flexible' were seen as inefficient or even disloyal to the team's success. Managers argued that these deviations were necessary to meet renewable energy targets, secure project bonuses, and avoid delays that cost hundreds of thousands of euros per day. As one HSE official admitted off the record, "If we followed all the rules strictly, we would never get anything done."

One day, a senior technician fell 8 metres while working alone on a tower, without a full second-party check. The fall was not fatal, but the investigation revealed systematic underreporting of near-misses, repeated violations of rest periods, and an informal culture of overruling among shift leaders. The media picked up the story, and NordTek's image as a "model HSE compliance" collapsed. Investors became suspicious, fines from regulators followed, and a top executive resigned. From the outside, NordTek looked like a reckless safety violator. Internally, the story was more complex: the deviation was a practical adjustment, a way to maintain productivity.

Setting up the next chapters

If we take Luhmann seriously, then safety is not a matter of adding more goals or better procedures. It's the improbable result of communication within and between operationally closed systems, each with its own way of seeing, deciding, and excluding.

The chapters that follow explore how systems construct meaning, manage risk, and create the appearance of order. Among other things, we'll look at:

- How decisions are framed and justified,
- How rules are bent, and why that often makes sense,
- And how systemic fragility hides behind institutional confidence.

If safety is a communication outcome instead of a fixed state, then it must be constantly made, remade, and reflected upon. Let's look at this theme of communication now.

Chapter 4 - Understanding the system's hearing problem

Keywords: Communication Thresholds, Selective Reception, Structural Coupling

Communication breakdown, it's always the same
Havin' a nervous breakdown, a-drive me insane
Communication Breakdown (Led Zeppelin)
Jimmy Page, John Paul Jones, John Bonham, 1969

Rethinking communication: It's harder than you think
Luhmann redefined communication. It's not just sending and receiving, like you and I might have learned from a management book. Communication is meaning-making, and meaning-making is fragile. For communication to work, three unlikely things must happen:

- A message is selected as information,
- It's disseminated, and,
- It's interpreted and understood.

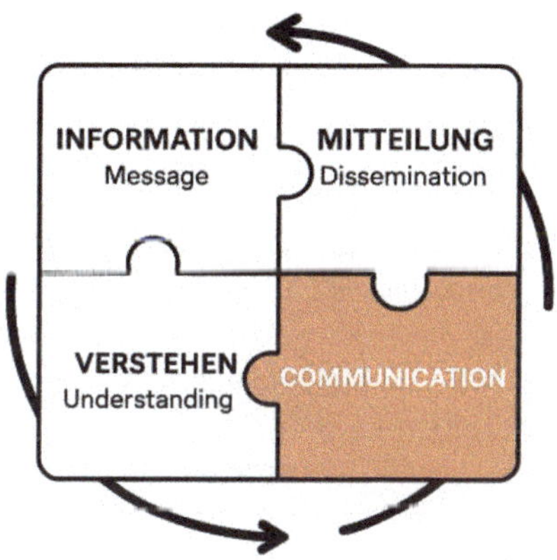

Luhmann's thresholds to communication

Miscommunication can occur at any stage. Even worse, 'improving' one of the puzzle pieces can make solving the puzzle harder. Luhmann didn't see misunderstanding as a failure; it's all part of the process.

"Humans cannot communicate, not even their brains can communicate, not even consciousness can communicate. Only communication can communicate". - Luhmann[32]

Organisations run on continuous communication instead of intention. Individuals are essential participants, but the organisation operates through codes, roles, and expectations, not private thoughts or emotions. Understanding organisations, then, requires focusing not on intentions or actions, but on communication itself as an autonomous process, like here:

When communication declared a tank safe[33]

On the evening of April 20, 2022, anchored off the coast of IJmuiden, the Netherlands, the chemical tanker NCC SAFA was being readied to receive a new load of gas oil. In the bow of the vessel, a deckhand climbed down into cargo tank 1SB to conduct a final visual inspection. It was a simple task, that had been performed many times before. He carried a flashlight, a radio, and the belief, unspoken but entrenched, that the tank was safe. It was not: Nitrogen, odourless and invisible, had seeped into the tank due to a valve that appeared closed but was, in fact, leaking. The oxygen level had dropped below the safe threshold. The tank had not been freshly tested, no Entry Permit had been issued, and no personal gas meter was worn. None of the protective layers defined in the procedures had been activated. To those aboard, the danger remained uncommunicated, because communication had already concluded: the tank was clean, the work was routine, the environment safe.

When the deckhand failed to respond, the first mate descended in after him. He, too, wore no gas meter. His action was not a calculated breach of protocol, but a nearly automatic response to help; influenced by life at sea, closeness among crew, and the knowledge that there was likely no one else nearby to intervene. Communication had failed to update itself, and so it repeated its previous declaration of safety, now lethally inaccurate. The crew was trained, the safety systems certified, the procedures known and posted throughout the vessel. The crew had even practiced emergency entry drills just two weeks earlier. But no message had interrupted the existing communication loop. The gas system's only physical safety barrier, a single manual valve, had failed internally. The tank had filled with nitrogen, and the system had no mechanism for detecting its own misbelief.

NCC SAFA in IJmuiden’s Harbour

Communication was procedural, manual, analog. The crew marked valve positions by hand on a control board. No sensors confirmed whether valves were truly closed or gas was still flowing. The entire system rested on human reporting embedded within a limited structure of feedback: visual inspections, maintenance intervals, and spoken confirmations over radio. The architecture of communication was formal but brittle.

In Luhmann’s systems-theoretical terms, what failed aboard NCC SAFA was not simply awareness, attention, memory, or skill. It was *communication's inability to unsettle itself*. The system reproduced a prior communication selection (‘the tank is safe’) without reinitiating the possibility of doubt. The risks were not reassessed because the logic of the previous Entry Permit still was used in daily routines.

The mate did not fall because he misjudged the risk, but because the system he operated within never re-entered doubt. It lacked redundancy, and checks at the edge of action. The oxygen meter alarm went off only after the rescue team entered; too late for prevention, just in time for classification... In the end, working safely failed because communication continued, uncorrected[34].

Your experience with the communication thresholds?
If you work in a complex organisation, you're probably very familiar with these thresholds in communication. For instance, safety reports often fail. Not because no one cares, but because the message fails at one of these stages, for instance in statements like these:

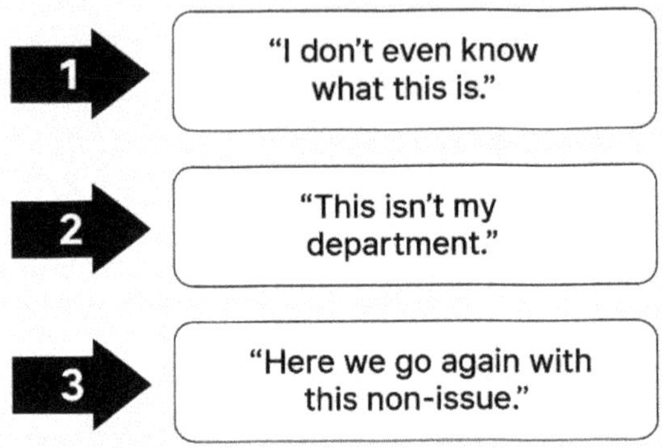

Practical examples of the three thresholds

What are the thresholds to communication in HSE?
Threshold 1: Communication Breakdown in Information Selection Phase
Threshold to overcome: There is a message with information.

A contractor receives a safety bulletin about a newly implemented lockout-tagout (LOTO) procedure. The bulletin uses complex terminology and lacks visuals or examples. The contractor misinterprets it as a general update rather than a change that requires immediate compliance. The contractor does not use the new LOTO procedure. Then there is an arc flash incident that injures a coworker. The message existed and was disseminated but was not understood. Both technical clarity and language appropriate for the target audience must be present.

Threshold 2. Communication Breakdown in the Dissemination Phase
Threshold to overcome: The message is disseminated.

An operator identifies a torn scaffold anchor point during a night shift and logs it into the digital inspection system. The alert does not trigger a notification to the day shift supervisor due to a missed software update. The day shift continues to work on the scaffolding, resulting in a near miss when the anchor fails. The message was entered into the correct channel, but the channel failed to transmit it as expected, due to a technical fault. This indicates a need to verify and monitor message flow integrity, not just message entry.

Threshold 3. Communication failure in the understanding phase
Threshold to overcome: The message has been understood and taken up as a basis for further communication or action.

A junior employee is concerned about excessive noise levels in a production area. The supervisor, who is used to the noise, dismisses it as 'normal factory environment' and takes no action. Long-term exposure leads to mild hearing loss in several employees and ultimately to legal sanctions for violations of noise standards. The message was understood and disseminated but not accepted as important or valid. The production system needs to be structurally linked to the risk management system to support meaningful action.

Recognising what your system can recognise
Luhmann helps us ask:
- When a safety issue is reported but not acted on, what really went wrong?
- Was the message even received?
- Was it recognised as relevant?
- Did it reach the right decision structure?
- Was it understood and accepted?

In HSE management, we want to keep improving what happens, including improving what our system can see happening. We can ask:
- What risks are communicable within your system's categories?
- What gets filtered out?
- Who or what defines 'what counts'?

Transition to Chapter 5: When distinctions break down
When an event doesn't fit any category, or worse, contradicts what the system believed was safe? This is where risk becomes a social event.

Chapter 5 – Entertain us: The ritual life of risk

Keywords: Alibi Risks, Risk Communication, Ritualisation of Safety, Reassurance

Here we are now, entertain us...
Smells Like Teen Spirit (Nirvana)
Kurt Cobain, Dave Grohl, Krist Novoselic, 1991

Risk prevention and the risk of prevention

In HSE management, we try to anticipate harm and act before it happens. We try to reduce the likelihood of unwanted events, or to minimise the consequences if they occur. We build our readiness against external, uncontrollable threats through training and reserves. We also use engineering standards, legal safeguards and insurance to enable risky decisions of our organisations by making them seem more manageable.

But Luhmann wrote[35] that prevention introduces new risks too. When we act to avoid one risk, we may create another. For instance:
- We detour traffic in order to work safely on the highway and get traffic jams in small villages with the associated risk for pedestrians and cyclists instead;
- We accept hidden costs of surveillance systems that undermine trust;
- We feel safe due to illusory controls.

In other words, the mechanisms meant to reduce uncertainty can themselves become sources of new, unacknowledged dangers.

Why do we manage the wrong risks?

Social systems often do not manage uncertainty by addressing primary risks directly. Instead, they give attention to more familiar, acceptable secondary risks. Luhmann[36] called these alibi risks[37]. These are surrogate risks that act as institutional substitutes. For example, instead of addressing the full complexity of systemic failure in a technical system, organisations focus on the risks of operator error or software failure. These are tangible, finite risks that can be 'managed'. In doing so, they avoid confronting the unmanageable. Accepting such risks is less about effectiveness than about restoring a sense of self-direction.
This pushing of risk into symbolic territory doesn't stop with decision-making. It also influences how organisations report,

display, and even imagine safety itself. The result is a stage-managed version of safety, where metrics and narratives line up with institutional comfort rather than operational reality.

The veil of silence and the invention of near misses
In business calculations, cost considerations reign supreme. The investment in safety prevention and health protection is a challenging venture, while the return on investment is not easy to quantify. Meanwhile, institutional legal health and safety requirements go together with rather different operational realities. What was meant to ensure workplace health and safety may become a façade, concealing problematic conditions behind a veil of silence.

Sociologist Ulrich Brinkmann[38] did research at an automobile manufacturing plant. At the front gate, there was a man-sized sign which proudly displayed the days elapsed since the last accident. A seemingly commendable practice, yet a different narrative unfolds. When questioned about the 'days since last accident' sign[39], the works council respond with a smile, and revealed that work accidents are being redefined or conveniently categorised as incidents involving remote workers. Others are asked to report to work despite injuries, distorting the reality behind the numbers. "This means we are the best in internal group benchmarking and don't jeopardise the existing level of our accident insurance contributions."

In the pursuit of a spotless safety record, the plant not only tolerated near misses but subtly encouraged making them up. "Part of this staging for benchmarking is that near misses have to happen. The logic is that by having them, we show we do avoid real accidents. Sometimes we therefore say: "Come up with a near miss"."

To understand how safety becomes symbolic, let's now explore how prevention itself can serve more to protect organisational legitimacy than to reduce actual harm.

Prevention as a political symbol

Symbolic prevention doesn't emerge in a vacuum. It's influenced by how organisations make, or avoid making, decisions. What looks like prevention on the surface is often the product of internal decision dynamics that turn even inaction into a choice.

The difference between external threats and our own risky decisions becomes strategic. Luhmann[40] gave the example of rocket tests in Lapland, where entire villages were evacuated by helicopter in order to prevent debris to fall on someone. The risk that something would happen during the evacuation per helicopter was more probable, but it was ignored or at least downplayed. So, what gets labelled as belonging to our own system versus belonging to the environment determines which problems receive attention. Ritualised prevention becomes a way to signal responsibility, even if it doesn't reduce real-world harm. As some prevention is symbolic, we have to watch for alibi risks: actions that feel safe but are structurally blind. This kind of prevention may reduce a primary risk, but it always creates the second-order risk of misplaced trust.

"*The risk of prevention is still a risk.*" – Luhmann[41]

So before celebrating prevention, ask:
- What uncertainty is this really addressing?
- What new risks are we silently accepting?
- Are we managing risk, or manufacturing reassurance?

To answer these questions, we must examine how decisions and non-decisions influence organisational risk management.

How organisations turn (non-)decisions into risk
Unlike broad societal systems like politics, economy, media, and law, organisations are distinct social systems with their own logic of communication and control. Organisations[42]:
- Have clear boundaries (member vs. non-member),
- Rely on formal decisions for their functioning,
- Operate through conditional memberships (you're in if you accept the internal rules of decision-making).

In organisations, everything becomes a decision:
- Forgot to order PPE? Your non-decision becomes a decision once consequences emerge.
- Ignored an environmental signal? Retroactively, that too is treated as a decision.

So, even silence or inaction can later be framed as "Someone decided not to act!" This creates a decision chain where past decisions influence current options, and present decisions anticipate future scrutiny. No action is ever fully neutral. This is how organisations, in Luhmann's words, generate themselves through *recursive decision-making*, not just through tasks or outcomes.
Because every decision could later be judged, organisations develop risk awareness next to their goal-seeking behaviour. They also become hyper-sensitive to anything that might later be seen as a failure. Bureaucracies are especially risk averse.

They aim for no surprises, maximum documentability, layered approvals and staged decisions (e.g., partial permits, and review loops). Organisations often react to primary uncertainty by spreading it out, by:

- Breaking a big risky decision into many small ones,
- Involving multiple stakeholders (to share blame), and
- Building formal processes that allow for defensibility over agility.

This is why checklists, forms, and rules are everywhere. They provoke decisions and limit improvisation. But they also have the risk of blinding systems to novelty or context. And that turns surprises into system failures.

An example of this comes from a fictionalised case, where safety procedures were technically in place but substantively absent.

The tank cleaning incident - No formal objection, but silent approval

A shutdown was scheduled at an industrial processing facility. One of the maintenance tasks was to have contractors clean an ethanol storage tank. The safety procedure for confined space entry was clear about the activities required:

- A signed permit,
- Atmospheric gas testing,
- Continuous monitoring, and
- Two-way communication.

Due to delays in the plant's maintenance schedule, pressure to gain time was slowly but surely mounting. The operations manager verbally suggested that preparations begin while the paperwork was being processed. The permit was pending and no one objected. The safety supervisor was off-site and had not signed. Contractors entered the tank and began their work, assuming they had tacit approval. Hours later, after a worker felt dizzy, it was discovered that the tank atmosphere had not been tested. Entry was stopped and fortunately no injuries were reported.

When the internal investigation began, the leading question was, "Who granted access without a permit?" Everyone pointed fingers at each other:

- The contractor said that the operations department had given the go-ahead verbally.
- Operations said that it was 'just preparation'.
- The safety supervisor said that they had never been formally consulted.

Yet the access occurred.

The organisation created risk not by one wrong decision, but by a series of partial, non-binding actions. A formal decision to grant access was never recorded, but the system behaved as if the decision had been made. This is what Luhmann meant by the term operational closure: each subsystem (safety, operations, contractor management, etc.) observed the situation through its own code, whether it was for compliance, efficiency, or progress. And each subsystem took local, defensible actions. But the absence of a decision was later reframed as a decision.

Luhmann would suggest that risk does not arise from a single transgression, but from the way decision structures are out of sync across codes. The retrospective attribution of decisions (Who is to blame?) serves the system's need to restore legitimacy, not necessarily to improve safety. HSE procedures may define formal thresholds, but socially distributed expectations and informal routines determine how risks actually accumulate.

When such decision chains multiply, they often give rise to a false sense of control. Systems appear rigorous but may be drifting into ritual.

The illusion of control
As organisational risk handling becomes more elaborate, confidence tends to increase: "We've checked everything!" But blind spots grow as well, since what doesn't fit the form is ignored. And after the fact, everything can still be reframed as a bad choice. This creates a loop of reassurance. The bureaucracy becomes excellent at *demonstrating* diligence, while potentially underestimating *emergent* risk.

"Uncertainty is reduced through collaborative decision-making or through project presentations by the stakeholders. Arguments are added to the initially favoured solution that make any residual risk seem tolerable. External resources, experts, externally acquired supplier reputations, or internal research may help absorb uncertainty. This can even lead to the illusion of having controlled risks before the decision. In any case, the effort expended here facilitates the demonstration of the greatest possible prudence and caution in the event that the decision is subsequently questioned." – Luhmann[43]

So, we don't just need to manage individual decisions. We have to observe how our organisations structure the *possibility* of decision. This means watching for how routines and forms both enable and constrain.
Remember: avoiding risk is itself risky, especially when systems overestimate their own foresight.

Some major industrial disasters show how even tightly controlled systems can miss critical threats. Not from lack of effort, but from how they structure observation.

Deepwater Horizon offshore drilling unit on fire[44] (2010)

The blowout that passed every test

In the months before the Deepwater Horizon explosion, BP completed hundreds of safety checks. Risk assessments had been filed, procedures followed, and assurance reports signed off. Everything appeared to be under control, until it wasn't. In hindsight, many asked: How could such a well-documented system fail so spectacularly? Luhmann might answer: *because the system confused checking with seeing.* Risk, in his view, is not just danger out there. It's how systems observe and fail to observe their own decision-making.

To fully grasp this transformation, we must not view risk as a technical quantity, but as a social construct embedded in organisational behaviour.

The social life of risk: From decisions to disputes

In traditional views of safety, risk is often framed as something to be identified, quantified, and controlled. But in complex organisations, Luhmann reminds us that *uncertainty is structurally embedded*. Systems generate their own risks by the very mechanisms they use to control them. Risk, in this sense, is not external danger but internal expectation: the anticipation of negative outcomes tied to decisions made under uncertainty. Organisations try to manage risk through checklists, controls, and formal processes. Yet these often fail to confront the real driver of failure: the selective blindness of the system itself.

But what happens when safety practices stop being inquisitive and instead become ceremonial?

When checking replaces seeing
Drew Rae and colleagues coined the term "probative blindness" [45]: a tendency for organisations to perform safety rituals such as audits, inspections, and risk assessments that appear to be empirical research but in reality, serve to confirm existing beliefs about safety. In disasters such as the Deepwater Horizon blowout, safety procedures were carried out by the book, but they functioned more as reassuring rituals than as tools for discovery.

Luhmann saw social systems such as organisations, teams, and supply chains as self-producing and self-referential. That is, they function by observing and reproducing their own processes, rather than relying on external input.
Luhmann deliberately distanced himself from a focus on individuals or simple cause-and-effect models. Instead, he viewed communication as the core activity that keeps social systems running[46]. From this perspective, knowledge and learning don't come from gaining access to an objective reality, but from how systems internally process and interpret events based on their own logic and distinctions. This insight reframes HSE challenges. Our problem is not ignorance, but how systems selectively construct what they consider 'known'.

Especially in complex environments, stability is not achieved through fixed structures, but through repeated processes that develop over time. Here we look not only at what happens, but also at how we observe and respond. This is particularly relevant in HSE management, where we want to gain insight into patterns in how incidents are reported, or risks are perceived. Systems are operationally closed but cognitively open: they process information based on their internal logic but continue to respond to their environment. This connection with the environment depends less on direct communication and more on timing and simultaneity. Think of how quickly a hazard is recognised and addressed relative to the moment it occurs.

There is no direct connection between individual thinking and the broader social system, for example the mindset of a safety officer versus the production facility. Instead, mutual influence occurs when both function in synchrony, such as when team members respond simultaneously to a shared safety signal, not necessarily through verbal communication.

Structures in a system only exist if they are communicated and adhered to. For example, a safety protocol 'exists' in practice only if it's known, adhered to and reinforced in communication. These structures are formed by the differences and expectations that are embedded in the organisational dialogue. Each system (a team, a department) retains its own logic, even in its interaction with other systems.

Rather than looking for separate explanations, it's important to observe how differences (for example between safe and unsafe practices, or between types of risk communication) influence the results. Paradoxes are not errors that we need to correct, but tools to think more creatively and deal more effectively with complexity. This does not require us to abandon existing safety models. It's about broadening the available perspectives and providing insight into how systems actually function and evolve.

Let's now turn to a public sector example, where symbolic safety practices are especially visible, yet often disconnected from operational outcomes.

The appearance of safety: Ritual, symbol, and exclusion in administrative practice

How do administrative systems produce the appearance of risk control while structurally excluding the conditions for substantive HSE management?

"Let's just organise a Safety Day again this year!"
In a public administration context, safety advisors, despite being nominally responsible for ensuring project safety, lacked formal training and instead focused their energies on organising highly visible but low-impact Safety Days. These events served more symbolic than functional purposes. The actual work of managing safe work was pushed to project teams who, often under time and resource pressure, generated documents that were ritualistic, designed to signal compliance rather than to ensure real-world safety outcomes. Meanwhile, the few critically skilled safety practitioners in the organisation found themselves structurally excluded from project communication flows; their inquiries remain unanswered, and access to project data was denied.

Luhmann explains how bureaucracies often engage in symbolic compliance; acts that are outwardly rational but inwardly disconnected from practical function. Safety plans often function similarly to what Luhmann describes as *decisions that are not real decisions* because they don't genuinely influence or regulate behaviour. They serve instead to maintain organisational legitimacy by producing signs of rationality. In an organisation where Safety Days were important, HSE management was abstracted to a point of harmlessness: pleasant, public-facing, and disconnected from system-critical functions.

System closure and exclusion
Luhmann's term *autopoietic systems* describes how systems reproduce their own elements and maintain boundaries. Safety-critical actors can be excluded beyond this boundary, because the organisation structurally selects whom to consider relevant. Communication structures in the system are functionally closed. This means that even critical feedback can be disregarded if it doesn't match the system's internal codes (e.g., project timelines, political optics, budgeting cycles).

Some systems don't expect actionable safety input; they expect symbolic confirmation of safety. Thus, critical experts, who provide inconvenient data or need project access, are excluded from the communication flow.
Luhmann pointed to the illusion of integration within complex organisations. The case above illustrates how functional roles (like 'safety advisor') are nominally integrated into administrative procedures but are not substantively integrated into decision-making. They serve more as 'organisational décor' than as operational assets.
What is seen is not what is operative; this divergence between formal structure and effective structure is central to Luhmann's analysis of modern administration. Behind these symbolic efforts lies a deeper issue: how organisations define decisions and what counts as action.

Decision as communication
Luhmann defines decisions not merely as acts but as communications that stabilise uncertainty. Plans can be produced, and safety can be discussed, but no real uncertainty is resolved. The system outputs artifacts (e.g., safety plans, and reports) without inputting or processing relevant risk information.
Luhmann wrote[47]: "The system performance of the administration is to process information into decisions."
If no relevant information enters, and no real decisions are made because they might disrupt political or managerial stability, then safety becomes a non-operationalised value.

This dynamic can manifest in several ways, as shown by Drew Rae and colleagues[48]:

- Analyses appear rigorous but systematically overlook real threats.
- Test results that raise concerns are dismissed as noise or anomalies.
- Bad news is held to higher standards of proof than good news.
- Models of risk are simplified until reality no longer fits.

In Luhmann's terms, these are failures of second-order observation; failures to observe how we observe. Organisations build feedback systems that filter out contradiction. Instruments are tuned to measure confirmation instead of disruption. In this way, safety tools become communication loops: they maintain confidence, but don't generate insight. In such feedback loops, even advanced safety tools can become instruments of self-confirmation rather than insight. So, what might it look like to design risk management that embraces discomfort, rather than avoids it?

To escape these closed loops, risk analysis must be reimagined as a form of disruptive observation:

- Promote scepticism instead of just compliance,
- Make space for unexpected or unwelcome results, and
- Treat uncertainty as meaningful, instead as an error to eliminate.

To find out if your organisation is stuck in reassurance mode, ask:

- Do our audits ever surface inconvenient results?
- Are we more comfortable validating safety than interrogating it?
- Who gets rewarded: those who challenge the system or those who echo it?

When safety systems close in on themselves, they risk losing the very openness that makes them effective. The solution is better distinctions. The implications are clear: when systems become self-referential, their safety practices serve more to reassure than to protect.

Transition to chapter 6

When organisations face complexity and uncertainty, they seek reassurance. Risk management then transforms from a mode of inquiry into a ritual of confirmation. These rituals are embedded in, and legitimised by, organisational procedures. These procedures *document and perform* safety. As we move from risk detection to institutional form, we begin to see that safety practices are symbolic too. They stabilise meaning, distribute trust, and signal legitimacy in the absence of consensus.

This brings us to a question: What makes safety procedures *feel* right, even when their connection to reality is questionable?

Chapter 6 – Form before function: Procedural safety

Keywords: Procedural Legitimacy, Safety Theatre, Symbolic Compliance

You can check out any time you like
But you can never leave
Hotel California (Eagles)
Don Henley, Don Felder, Glenn Frey, 1976

Introduction - Why follow rules you disagree with?
Safety rules can feel overly bureaucratic or disconnected from practical work. Luhmann wrote:
"In modern society, legitimacy is not achieved by content, but by procedure." [49]

"Do we really need to wear our safety helmet on the whole plant, including the offices? Why?"[50]

Procedures reduce complexity by creating predictability. Compliance is less about conviction, and more about trust in the form. Safety checks, certifications, and audits function like rituals. They don't guarantee outcomes but produce the appearance of control and legitimacy.

Procedures allow actors to act despite disagreement, doubt, or ignorance. In safety, this is especially relevant: decisions must be made without omniscience.
In earlier societies, legitimacy relied on shared values or religious truth. Modern systems (e.g., law, safety, administration) rely on procedural justice instead. Even flawed procedures maintain legitimacy as long as they are followed consistently.

Procedural legitimacy in practice
A week before the external audit, the plant was buzzing with last-minute preparations. Inspection routes were run through trial runs, documents were updated with retroactive signatures, and outdated signage was replaced overnight. Some training records were reconstructed after an internal memo urged everyone to "check for gaps." Everyone knew the routine.

"Let's make sure everything is in order," the HSE manager said in the preparatory meeting, without a hint of irony. No one asked what "in order" meant. It didn't matter whether the process maps reflected practice. It didn't matter whether anyone had read the emergency plan. What mattered was that everything looked audit ready. This illustrates a central theme. The point was never lining up with expectation instead of reality. Procedure had replaced meaning.

On the day of the inspection, the auditor arrived, was greeted warmly at the gate, led through the maintenance backlog, and shown a carefully prepared safety board, covered in laminated slogans and color-coded graphics. A production technician whispered to me, "This board is updated once a year, for this day."

The audit went smoothly. A few minor nonconformities were noted. The team breathed a collective sigh of relief.
Afterward, in the break room, someone joked, "I wish we ran the factory like we pretend." There was laughter, not cynical, just tired.

The audit revealed no safety issues. But it didn't reveal much either. Everyone complied. Everyone knew it was a performance. And yet no one suggested skipping the next audit. It was still important. Not because it improved safety, but because it confirmed that the organisation was doing something; something visible, procedural, legitimate. The audit was a ritual of reassurance. It didn't guarantee safety, but it helped the system maintain its image of control. In Luhmann's words, it provided legitimacy without agreement, compliance without conviction. This is the heart of procedural legitimacy. The appearance of diligence becomes more important than the substance of discovery.

These symbolic rituals don't emerge randomly. They follow a systemic logic of communication under conditions of complexity and mistrust.

Audits, permits, certifications - The rituals of HSE management

Audits, permits and certifications are both tools for attempted control and rituals of trust. They generate accountability and symbolic reassurance more than actual certainty. Safety Culture Maturity Models, for example, often act more as performance of care than as diagnosis of practice. More about that, later. But why do such rituals persist, even when everyone involved sees through them? The answer lies in how modern systems construct fairness itself.

Fairness is performative

Fairness is not about equal outcomes but about credible process. In the safety domain, this explains the persistent use of incident reviews and hazard assessments, even when their direct impact is unclear. Procedure trumps truth.

In complex systems:
- outcomes are uncertain,
- values are plural, and
- facts are contested.

Procedures offer a stable middle. Not quite truth, not quite belief, but a performative mechanism of reassurance. But they filter out a lot. And that filtering is structural. Procedures are more than tools for control; they influence what is seen as controllable.

So how do procedures influence communication in safety management systems, and what do they exclude by design?

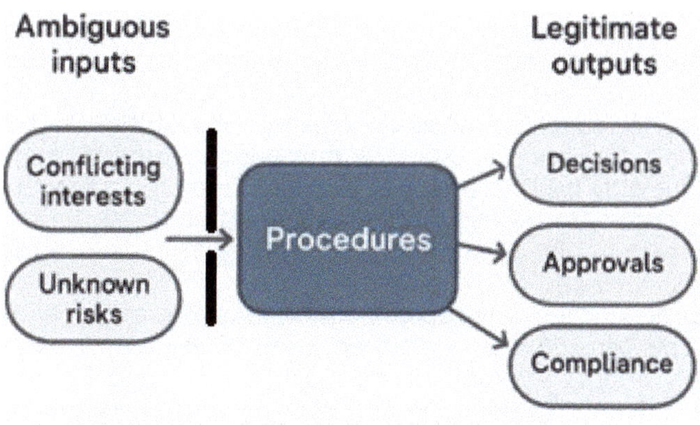

Procedures as communication filter

How do we understand compliance and formality in HSE?
Luhmann saw compliance and formality not as bureaucratic burdens, but as mechanisms to create trust in systems that are too complex to be fully transparent or observable. This is not a failure of logic, but a *strategic simplification*. Trust becomes distributed across the form, even when the content is weak. According to Luhmann, procedures are means to create legitimacy under conditions of structural ignorance. Of course, it's not the case that nothing can ever go wrong in a bureaucracy, but legitimacy comes from the credibility of the processes by which decisions are made. Procedures signal fairness, impartiality and continuity in contexts where direct control or full understanding is impossible. In this sense, formal structures help to stabilise expectations and mediate trust between differentiated and interdependent subsystems.

Sidney Dekker criticised the procedural orientation of the safety bureaucracy with its checklists, audits and compliance mechanisms that are often disconnected from the reality of safe working. According to Dekker[51], compliance promotes ritualised care that crowds out adaptation by experienced workers and erodes the autonomy of professionals. Where Luhmann sees procedures as pillars of trust in complex systems, Dekker sees them as a brake on resilience and a barrier to restoring human-centred safety. Luhmann places trust in the architecture of communicative structures and asks how legitimacy is maintained when systems can't know everything. Dekker asks how organisations can reconnect with the practical wisdom of those doing the work; what actually happens, not what compliance systems imagine should happen. However, Luhmann's approach to procedures is essential *for the realities of high-risk domains*, where central coordination and formal structures are needed[52]. When risks must be shared across multiple actors and time periods, structured procedures form the basis for collective decision-making, accountability, and escalation. Luhmann shows why bureaucracy persists and how it can not only be tolerated but also deployed to support trust and legitimacy in times of uncertainty and high-risk.
While procedures can support trust and legitimacy in complex systems, they can also create blind spots. This is especially true when procedural forms replace continuous interaction with real work. This tension is exacerbated when safety management suddenly adopts the logic of the market, as evidenced by the change towards outsourcing and contract-based coordination at a government agency for public works, transportation, and water management.

How market logic can blind systems to risk

- Why did risk management deteriorate after outsourcing?
- Why did technical experts feel excluded?
- Why did project failures increase despite clear contracts?

Safety professionals and managers in government organisations may ask themselves these questions when looking back at the Dutch 'the market, unless' policy[53]. The idea was simple: let the market handle design and execution through integrated contracts, so that the government can focus on oversight.

But this led to unexpected consequences at the Dutch agency for public works:

- Technical staff reported being cut off from site visits and live project feedback.
- Expertise became internalised and abstract; assessments took place on paper, not in context.
- Communication between risk-aware actors and decision makers was disrupted.

Instead of managing risks adaptively, risks were pre-allocated through contracts. This change from relational to transactional coordination made real-time adjustments more difficult. Legal safeguards replaced technical dialogue. Trust gave way to formal distance. Instead of enabling coordination, formal structures created distance. The procedures were intact, but the feedback loops were broken.

In Luhmann's terms, the change altered the structural coupling between *governance* and the *market*. The two systems no longer co-produced decisions in real time. The governance system withdrew from continuous observation, which created a blind spot in communication. How did this affect the functioning of the system? Project coordination suffered from delays and higher failure costs. Embedded learning from experts in the field was lost. The organisation became less reflexive; less able to observe how it observes. An external evaluation led to reappraisal. It made clear that outsourcing execution is not the same as outsourcing observation or adaptation. To function safely, a system must maintain operational coupling, communicative connections between design, implementation, and governance. "Market unless" led to a reduction in second-order observation; the ability to reflect on others' perceptions of risk. The solution was to reconnect the system. Not only through new policies, but also through new communication loops that restore visibility to the real work. After all, what an organisation can't observe, it can't manage.

In response to these issues, reforms are often introduced. But paradoxically, these reforms can reinforce the procedural traps they seek to dissolve.

The bureaucracy trap: Why reform often adds rules
Attempts to reform public systems by introducing market mechanisms often lead not to leaner operations but to layered bureaucracy. Luhmann's student Stefan Kühl notes[54], "through competitiveness, you get a double bureaucratic process": one to monitor goal achievement, and another to ensure compliance with the unchanged regulations. This paradox is familiar in the world of HSE management[55]. For instance, efforts to streamline safety through lean systems frequently result in more audits, more checklists, and more documentation, each introduced to demonstrate control and accountability. So, reforms aimed at agility can produce more layers of surveillance. The system doubles down on reassurance. Safety audits may aim to reduce inefficiency, but they often multiply procedural layers, focusing attention on form completion rather than risk awareness. Compliance checklists promise standardisation but can displace real reflection with box-ticking. What looks like simplification becomes complexity in disguise. This reveals a deeper truth: procedural legitimacy is not about speed or simplicity, but about ensuring decisions are resilient, contestable, and fair. In complex systems, the appearance of efficiency can mask an expanding infrastructure of control, justified by reform, but driven by mistrust.

An important example of symbolic communication is 'safety culture', a term that has become less about explanation and more about branding in recent years.

Safety Culture as a symbolically generalised communication medium
Function systems like the economy, law, and politics operate through symbolically generalised communication media such as money, power, and law. In the *economic system*, communication is generalised through payment/non-payment distinctions.

"The economy communicates not about values, but through payments." - Luhmann[56]
In other words, when safety culture is commodified, the focus moves from meaning or truth to exchangeability.
Safety culture lives in a market of meaning, sustained by consultants, models, and metrics.

The safety culture industry as a self-referential system
An example of procedural legitimacy outsourced to the market, is the safety culture audit. In Jean-Christophe Le Coze's view[57], safety culture has become a medium of exchange within a market of ideas. It enables consultants, companies, and regulators to communicate legitimacy, responsibility, and improvement, not through operational safety outcomes per se, but through recognizable programmes and certifications. The *safety market* does not need to prove actual safety outcomes to maintain its operation, only to reproduce communications that are accepted within its own code (e.g., *'culture maturity', 'psychometric scores',* etc.).

In Luhmann's view, this is not surprising, in a functionally differentiated system, it's more important that something remains connectable within the system than whether it's true. What makes these cultural products so attractive is their simplicity. But this clarity comes at a price: a loss of depth and context.

Reduction of complexity through simplified cultural products
Luhmann insists that all communication systems work by reducing complexity, *not* by capturing reality in its entirety, but by rendering only selected aspects communicable.
Le Coze's critique of simplistic 'culture products' (models, assessments) shows how complex organisational realities are reduced to fit marketable forms. These forms are easier to audit, regulate, and sell, but they eliminate the heterogeneity, conflict, and ambiguity that make safety meaningful. This corresponds with Luhmann's principle:
"Meaning reduces complexity by presenting a world as meaningful." — Luhmann[58]

If we step back, we see that 'safety culture' often works less as a reflection of real conditions and more as a mechanism to *imagine a safer world*.

Safety culture as a fictional expectation generator

Luhmann distinguishes between factual expectations based on past outcomes and counterfactual or symbolic expectations, which enable action despite uncertainty.

The safety culture promoted by consultants, functions as a symbolic expectation structure. It offers fictional stability in complex, high-risk environments where real predictability is impossible. In this view, safety culture is not necessarily wrong: it's structurally useful fiction. It generates orientation and coordination in the absence of direct control.

But these symbolic systems face a critical challenge, and that is translation. What is meaningful in one domain may be meaningless or counterproductive in another.

The blind spot of systemic translation

Le Coze points to a major empirical blind spot: how are safety culture models *actually translated* into practice? Luhmann would describe this as the incommensurability between systems: what is meaningful in the consulting subsystem (saleable frameworks) may be non-translatable or meaningless in the local, operational context of the organisation. It's no surprise, then, that maturity models have come under scrutiny. Their appeal lies in their neatness, not necessarily in their insight.

Safety culture maturity revisited

Safety culture maturity models have gotten a lot of critique lately. These models reward performative gestures by means of policy language, reporting structures, and feedback loops. Meanwhile, they fail to assess whether risk is being meaningfully engaged with at all levels. For instance, a Safety Culture Ladder might document how often near-misses are reported. But does it reveal if those reports are taken seriously, or whether silence is safer than disclosure?

It may count the number of safety observations. But does it show whether those observations prompt change, or whether they're done to fulfil quotas?

Organisations manage impressions of how they manage risk, rather than just managing it. The safety theatre is not a *failure of culture*, but an artifact of complexity. Rather than dismantle the theatre entirely, we might do better to pull back the curtain. Invite backstage voices into the dialogue. Explore informal routines, jokes, and silences. Begin to observe not just what is performed, but what is possible.

Safety Theatre: Performing assurance, hiding contradiction
Who looks carefully at the everyday life of organisations, might quickly find out that safety isn't just practiced, but it's performed too. Stefan Kühl used the metaphor of "Theatre", a stage on which various organisational actors play symbolic roles. Inspired by this, here's the "Safety Theatre"[59]:

The Safety Theatre

The Safety Theatre features:
- a cheerful frontline worker in high-visibility PPE,
- a confident HSE manager holding up a 'Zero Harm' script, and
- the quiet whispers behind the curtain: reminders of economic priorities, time pressure, and organisational fatigue.
- Somewhere in a corner of the stage, hazards are quite literally swept under the rug.

In the Safety Theatre, roles are clear, risks are staged, and the audience is the organisation's external environment.
This visual scene captures an important dynamic in modern organisations: the disconnect between espoused values and enacted realities. The performance is not deceitful by intention. It's a social ritual; a way to maintain legitimacy, deflect

scrutiny, and sustain the illusion of control in environments where control is partial, and uncertainty is ever-present.

Now we could make fun of this and move on. But then we would miss something important. Because Luhmann called this kind of communicative decoupling *a functional necessity* in complex systems. Organisations *need* to reduce internal friction, meet external expectations, and uphold a sense of order. Especially when outcomes can't be guaranteed. This creates a strong incentive to focus on being seen to do safety, rather than confronting the more difficult question of how safety is made meaningful in practice.

The Safety Pub Quiz is a gamified alternative to the traditional toolbox meeting in the Dutch construction and infrastructure sector[60]. It transforms standard content on occupational safety into an interactive group quiz. For 90 minutes, participants work on important safety topics, guided by a quizmaster and a safety expert, covering the same material as in conventional toolbox sessions.

The Pub Quiz is designed to meet the formal requirements for safety training in the context of the Dutch Construction & Infrastructure collective labour agreement. The format allows companies to mark the session as an official safety meeting and at the same time offer a more engaging and socially dynamic experience. What the Pub Quiz does, is communicating about safety. What it delivers is a specific form of self-description of the organisation: "We take safety seriously and make it fun!" This signals compliance, but not necessarily risk reduction.

In the pub quiz, safety functions as a *symbolic generalisation*. It enables organisations to communicate across roles and functions (managers, the people on site, inspectors) using a shared form, even if the meanings differ. In this way, safety becomes a sign of participation. Changing the system is not intended.

An important function of the Pub Quiz is that it's considered an official toolbox meeting; it thus meets a legal requirement. The organisational system and the legal system are structurally linked: a form (the quiz) translates the organisational communication into something that meets the binary code of the law (legal/illegal). The logic of the checkboxes ("we did the toolbox") is retained, even if the format is changed. Safety communication here serves to reduce legal risks, not necessarily operational risks.

Furthermore, the game format introduces playful semantics into safety, making it 'fun'. In Luhmann's terms, a subsystem within the organisation uses a recreational code (fun/boring) to process a functional imperative (safety). This can increase attention and engagement but also carries the risk of trivialisation. The semantic shift from 'danger' to 'points won' can reduce the urgency that risk requires.

Admittedly, the quiz is a clever way to refresh routines and stimulate reflexivity. But unless it leads to new decision-making starting points (e.g. changing the way work is organised, hazards are limited, or power is distributed), it's communicating about safety without changing the risk.

Luhmann would also ask: Who owns this communication system? Does every participant in the Pub Quiz understand the content, or is participation just a pretence? If some people do not participate or if certain participants don't speak the language (e.g. migrant workers with limited Dutch), then this is symbolic inclusion and not functional communication.
So, what does all this mean? Not that such rituals are useless, but that we must understand what they actually do, and what they can't.
In conclusion, Luhmann would not find the Pub Quiz unimportant, but he would find it rather performative than transformative. The system considers itself safe and that observation is the "safety", nothing more. Luhmann would classify it under the domain of safety theatre, which reassures the organisation about its own moral position and at the same time makes it comply with procedural laws and regulations and reputation. What is missing is the link between the operation and the scientific and technical systems that would actually make the work safer.

Transition to chapter 7

This chapter showed how procedures, audits, and rituals can create the appearance of safety, even in the absence of meaningful risk engagement. But form alone doesn't explain how HSE management actually functions or fails. To understand that we must turn to the more fragile infrastructure: the interaction of power, trust, and dissent. Influence without authority, trust without scrutiny, and procedures without disruption can all stabilise systems, but they can also blind them. In the next chapter, we'll explore how power functions as communication, how trust both enables and endangers, and why constructive distrust may be one of the most important forces in keeping responsive. When it comes to HSE, what holds the system together is often carefully managed tension.

Chapter 7 – Power, trust, and HSE management systems

Keywords: Power as Communication, Constructive Distrust, Useful Illegality

Been beat up, battered 'round
Been sent up, and I've been shot down
You're the best thing that I've ever found
Handle me with care.
Handle With Care (Travelling Wilburys)
George Harrison, 1988

Now that we've seen how form can replace function in HSE management systems, we must ask: what happens when organisations try to inject emotion and morality into this procedural logic?

The so-called culture of active care
A recurring theme in safety writing and consultancy is the 'culture of active care'[61]. Consultants inspire organisations to 'create a culture of care'. Luhmann reminds us that organisations are not moral beings, nor are they capable of 'care' in the human sense of the word. Care is a psychological or interactional concept, whereas organisations are autopoietic communication systems[62]. What appears to be 'care' from the outside is a pattern of internal communication that follows organisational codes (e.g. efficient/inefficient, compliant/non-compliant). The appeal to empathy, leadership and commitment to safety by external consultants would be seen by Luhmann as an attempt to reprogramme the organisation's communication, not as a transformation of its 'culture'. What looks like moral progress may in fact be a rebranding of existing structures, with new slogans but old tendencies.

Attempts to create a 'culture of care' assume that values and attitudes can be deliberately influenced through training, leadership models and incentives. Luhmann was sceptical about this. Systems reproduce themselves through communication, not through shared values or human intentions. The idea that a unified 'culture' can be created ignores the fact that organisations are subject to multiple contexts in which multiple logics (e.g. safety, productivity, finance) coexist and conflict. A moral vocabulary (empathy, involvement, compassion) would be seen by Luhmann as a symbolically generalised communication tool that attempts to mobilise attention but can't fully direct systemic activities.

Luhmann would ask: What is the functional code of 'safety' within the organisation? Is it risk/safety? Responsible/irresponsible? Control/ deviation? He would probably note that promoting care changes the code from technical or legal distinctions to a moral dichotomy (caring/not caring). This can be useful in creating resonance, but it also creates new blind spots. After all, emotional appeals can obscure structural causes of harm. "Actively caring" can degenerate into a performance if it's not structurally supported. This performance might create the appearance of

> commitment. But it masks deeper limitations in how safety is embedded within organisational codes.
>
> Often advocates of a caring culture advocate for behaviour change through personal ownership and emotional involvement. Luhmann warns that complexity is not solved by goodwill. Even well-intentioned interventions will have unintended consequences, interact unpredictably with other subsystems (e.g., law, finance, and HR), and will also be interpreted differently depending on the observer (e.g., manager, auditor, and employee). We might say, "The corridor to hell is paved with motivational posters."
>
> From a systems theory perspective, 'caring' could be reframed as a risk management strategy. It provides an alibi risk (symbolic prevention) that reassures stakeholders. Through this, employees feel heard, and leaders feel responsive. Furthermore, supervisors see visible effort. But the question Luhmann would ask is: does this reduce the real risk, or does it merely stabilise expectations?

If care is not a stable organising principle in systems, then what is? For Luhmann, the answer lies in a different kind of coordination: power, understood as communicative influence.

Power without coercion: Influence and trust in safety systems

A safety officer halts operations due to ambiguous signals. Some colleagues grumble, a few question the need, but the decision stands. There's no punishment for disobedience, yet no one disobeys. Why? The answer isn't fear. It's something subtler: trust, legitimacy, structure. The officer doesn't impose control, but influences expectations. Luhmann invites us to see this as communication instead of coercion. In complex systems, power isn't something you wield but it's something you participate in.

Power as communication

Niklas Luhmann redefines power as a symbolically generalised communication medium. In his view, power is the ability to have decisions accepted instead of *enforced*. Power structures which communications are meaningful: what can be said, what gets heard, and what leads to action.

"Power is not control. It is communication"[63] – Luhmann

This different framing shows us the interactions and recognitions. This is especially relevant in HSE management systems, where authority often depends on trust and role clarity. In this light, power becomes fragile and contingent. It exists only if recognised. Once refused, it collapses. In HSE management, this explains why influence often depends more on role structure and trust than on command chains.

The anatomy of influence

Luhmann distinguishes between several forms of influence:

- Power is time-generalised influence. It stabilises expectations across changing situations.
- Authority is topic-generalised influence. It comes with formal roles and is context dependent.
- Leadership is socially generalised influence. It mobilises trust and reframes uncertainty.

These are broadly relational instead of purely hierarchical. It's not just what is said in high-risk environments, but who can say it, and when it resonates, that determines effectiveness. Power helps reduce complexity by closing down options, authority signals what is expected, and leadership creates space for redefinition. In high-stakes environments, this interaction allows for fast decisions under uncertainty. Without these communicative tools, every choice would require full negotiation. Imagine a safety-critical decision without any structure: every step contested; every risk re-evaluated. This is paralysing. Power, in systems theory, exists to enable communication by narrowing possibilities. It makes collective action possible by reducing the range of what needs to be discussed at every turn. This kind of influence is about framing what counts as legitimate discourse. And that is precisely what systems need to function: a way to filter relevance and stabilise meaning. But power alone is not enough. For influence to stick, trust must carry it forward, especially when uncertainty is high and time is limited.

Trust: The invisible foundation

Power without trust quickly turns into resistance. Luhmann described trust as a way of managing uncertainty[64].
Trust allows communication to proceed without full knowledge. In HSE management, decisions often need to be made before all information is available. Trust enables forward motion. It substitutes for proof, and it allows 'good enough' to be acted upon without delay.

Without trust, systems slow down or fragment. But with too much trust, new risks can arise. We now turn to that paradox. Power structures communication, but trust gives it momentum. When power loses trust, its function collapses. It's no longer recognised. Organisational roles offer a partial solution, because they stabilise influence by formalising it. But this only works if the structure is recognised and maintained.

Role legitimacy: Power tied to structure
In organisations, power is rarely personal. It flows through roles, procedures, and expectations. A safety professional may not have executive rank, but if their role is tied to clear decision programmes (e.g. reporting lines, permits, protocols) their influence becomes durable. Organisations can't function unless they define what need not be known.
Formalisation frees individuals from having to justify their authority at every turn. It allows roles to carry decisions. This is why even contested procedures are often followed; they create the appearance and function of rationality. Yet many HSE professionals operate without formal power. Their success hinges on translation; making safety legible within the language of leadership.

Managing up: Influence without authority
Many safety professionals face the challenge of influencing senior leaders without formal power. Success often depends on what Luhmann calls '*Anschlussfähigkeit*', connectability.

To manage up, we have to:
- Speak in system-relevant codes (e.g., financial risk, legal exposure, brand reputation).
- Time interventions strategically (e.g., after incidents or during review cycles).
- Frame proposals as continuity instead of disruption (e.g., "Here's a safer way to meet your goal.")

The trick is not to demand attention but to make safety communicable in the terms the system already values. In practical terms, this means:
- Translating safety risks into legal, financial, or reputational terms.
- Avoiding moralising language that isolates decision-makers.
- Proposing adjustments, not just objections.
- Demonstrating an understanding of the system's internal logic.

When a HSE professional translates a hazard into 'potential operational downtime' rather than 'ethical violation', they show their strategic advisory capacity. Communication succeeds when it resonates within the receiver's framework. Influence, in this sense, is adapted instead of imposed. Power flows not from position, but from corresponding strategically. But trust is not always examined. In many cases, it becomes self-reinforcing, sustaining legitimacy even when insight is lacking.

Reflexive trust and symbolic performance

In many organisations, trust is reflexive: we trust someone because the system does. Trust becomes a performance that reinforces itself. This is efficient but dangerous. It can lead to symbolic compliance rather than genuine scrutiny. Procedure replaces truth with trust in the form. This is why procedures don't guarantee safety; they guarantee *legitimacy*. Safety becomes something that looks right, rather than something that necessarily *is* right. This soft form of power allows organisations to function under complexity. But it also highlights their fragility. Especially when legitimacy is presumed, not earned.

Power as possibility instead of control

Power, in Luhmann's systems theory, is not domination, but rather the possibility of coordination under complexity. For HSE professionals, this means acting not as enforcers, but as conductors of system awareness. The goal is not to impose behaviour, but to structure expectations so that safe, healthy, and environmentally friendly alternatives become the most plausible path.

The authority to stop work, to challenge decisions, to escalate concerns, only function if accepted by the system. They depend on trust, structure, and timing. Influence, then, is powerful because it's recognised. This *soft skill* is far from *weak*. Power without coercion is the everyday reality of organisational life. And in HSE management, it's often the most important kind.

If trust enables systems to move, then constructively applied distrust keeps them honest. Luhmann saw distrust not as dysfunction, but as a necessary tension.

Constructive distrust: When systems challenge themselves

> ***From trust to trouble***
> A major petrochemical refinery had long prided itself on its open reporting culture. "We trust our people," the safety director said. "And they trust us." Survey scores confirmed it; so did low incident rates. But when a known leak near a catalytic reactor led to an unplanned shutdown, the follow-up revealed something unsettling: several operators had noticed the issue weeks earlier but said nothing. Why? Because they trusted that someone else had already acted.
> "Raising it again just felt like noise," one technician said. "I assumed they had it under control."
>
> In complex systems, trust can be too efficient. When everything seems in order, questions feel disruptive. But safety needs friction as it doesn't emerge from harmony alone.

This case illustrates that the absence of disagreement isn't always a sign of strength. It may rather be a warning that the system has stopped listening to itself.

Distrust as a functional mechanism

Niklas Luhmann described distrust not as a failure of social bonds, but as an alternative strategy for managing complexity. In systems terms, distrust can:

- Redirect attention,
- Create redundancy,
- Build slack, and
- Slow down premature consensus.

Distrust simplifies complexity through withdrawal, resistance, and redundancy.

> After the refinery incident, a group of senior technicians formed an unofficial 'red team'. They questioned assumptions, double-checked reports, and maintained their own shadow checklists. Management initially resisted: wasn't this a breach of trust?
>
> But the team uncovered several hidden vulnerabilities, including a gas sensor logging faulty data. What seemed like scepticism turned into a system-saving asset.

Too much cohesion can backfire. Trust becomes performative, and silence becomes a rational strategy.

Challenging the harmony bias

Organisations often equate trust with unity. Dissent gets framed as negativity. But in reality, too much trust can lead to silence:

- People assume concerns have already been handled.
- Raising doubts is seen as "You're not being a team player."

- Dissent gets self-censored in favour of perceived cohesion.

This is what Luhmann would call a self-reinforcing loop of selective perception. Trust becomes symbolic: a signal of loyalty rather than a basis for scrutiny. Constructive distrust interrupts this loop. It reframes dissent not as threat, but as contribution. The challenge, then, is to separate destructive friction from productive tension. Not all distrust is helpful, but some of it is essential.

Distrust done well

Distrust can, of course, be destructive when it becomes paranoid or cynical. But when it's cultivated with care, it sharpens attention and increases systemic resilience.

Productive forms of distrust are:
- Extra checks on assumptions (redundancy),
- Allowing time to question decisions (slack), and
- Pushing back on automated or symbolic procedures (resistance).

Destructive forms of distrust are:
- No decision is good enough (paralysis),
- Distrust of people rather than systems (blame-seeking), and
- Undermining coordination by withholding information.

The goal, then, is to balance trust with some *constructive distrust*. The deeper value of distrust lies in its capacity to sharpen a system's reflexes. It opens space for second-order observation.

From emotional friction to systemic tension

One of Luhmann's great insights was that systems thrive on tension, not just agreement. A risk-aware organisational culture channels discomfort without silencing it. It uses second-order observation to ask not just "what went wrong," but "how did we stop seeing risk?"

Constructive distrust, in this frame, is a corrective mechanism. It forces the system to pause, re-evaluate, and adapt.

In the refinery, the unofficial red team did more than raising a red flag:
- They built tools,
- They created a parallel checklist for high-risk processes,
- They cross-checked log data against physical observations, and
- They insisted on rotating auditors, to avoid local bias.

At first, this was met with scepticism. But after they identified a critical instrumentation fault, one that had passed three internal audits, leadership changed its view. The red team was formally integrated into the plant's hazard review process. Distrust became design. The system learned to include its own critics.

What does this mean for practice? For those working in or around safety systems, supporting constructive distrust becomes a leadership task.

Implications for HSE professionals

For HSE leaders and practitioners, the lesson is clear: Harmony without scrutiny is a liability. To support constructive distrust:
- Legitimise dissent: Create roles or forums for challenging assumptions;
- Recognise shadow practices: Don't penalise extra vigilance, but learn from it;
- Surface informal checks: These often signal gaps in formal systems; and
- Be reflexive about your risk models: Ask not just "Is this safe?" but "How do we know this is safe?"

Adaptive friction as a feature

Complex systems don't stay safe through passive compliance. They adapt, question, and correct. Trust enables communication, but distrust, properly directed, keeps systems honest. Luhmann's theory helps us see distrust not as a social failure, but as a functional necessity. It's the counterpart to power-as-communication: a way for systems to self-monitor, to create internal variation, and to resist their own blind spots. Constructive distrust is care made visible. It's not disloyal, but critically exercised responsibility. This perspective contrasts sharply with a lot of mainstream management thinking about trust and openness, which often overlooks the systemic dynamics that Luhmann makes visible.

A living system map

The relationships between structure, trust, and distrust form a dynamic system of interaction. An ongoing tension generates new systemic capacities.

The map below[65] is a living representation of how organisations function under complexity. Where structure, trust, and distrust converge, an *HSE Adaptive System* emerges. This adaptive system coordinates action through influence, sustains scrutiny through resilience, and maintains legitimacy through safe operation. The overlapping zones illustrate how core system-level properties arise from procedural clarity, relational trust, and critical reflexivity. So, working safely arises from the productive tension between trust and constructive challenge. Systems that integrate both authority and scepticism become capable of adaptation.

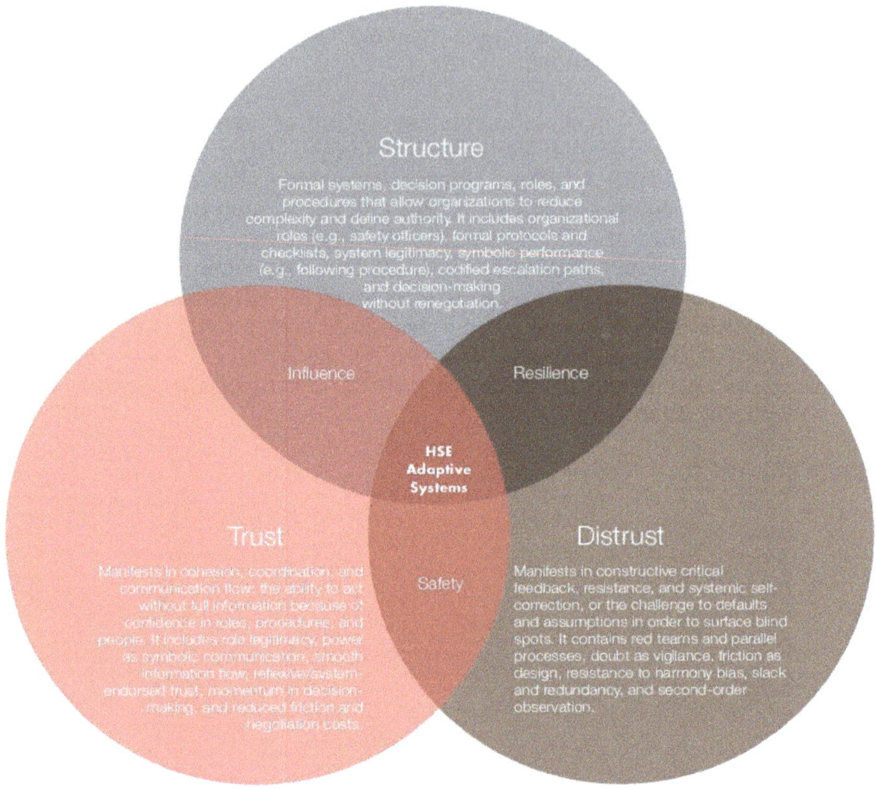

Trust Map - Map 1 Frame 1 3

VenningMachine.com

Constructive distrust versus popular management books on trust and psychological safety

Most contemporary management literature on leadership (e.g. Amy Edmondson's books) see *trust* and *psychological safety* as the foundations of a mature safety culture. The authors generally assume:

- Trust as a precondition for speaking up;
- Psychological safety as the absence of fear in interactions;
- The role of leadership in modelling openness, care and consistency; and
- A progression from compliance, to commitment, to care, where people feel safe to report and reflect.

The central assumption is that fear silences people and trust enables the truth. Where these management authors see silence as fear, Luhmann sees it as misplaced confidence. The danger isn't just that people won't speak up, but that they think they don't need to.

The harmony bias challenged by Luhmann
Luhmann has the same foundation of trust but adds a system-level insight: trust alone is not enough. In highly trusted, cohesive teams or organisations, a new risk arises. People don't remain silent out of fear, but out of a, sometimes misplaced, confidence that others can handle it.
This introduces a harmony bias; the tendency of well-functioning systems to filter out discomfort, dissent, or redundancy in the name of cohesion. The refinery case above shows how excessive trust can lead to collective inaction, despite high scores for psychological safety.

What is needed is to balance trust and scepticism. Where mainstream advice promotes emotional openness, Luhmann encourages cognitive resistance to overconfidence. Where others encourage relationship-centred care, he advocates systems-centred reflexivity. For him, dissent is not disloyalty but a sign of responsibility, a visible concern. The Eternit case illustrates these ideas. It shows how systemic blind spots persist, even when organisations follow the rules and broadcast moral commitment.

Eternit and the systemic limits of safety[66]

Eternit was a Dutch producer of asbestos fibres. When the production of asbestos was banned in the Netherlands in 1993, the company switched to the production of cement fibres. Eternit, like any formal organisation, operated on the basis of decisions that lead to further decisions. The organisation described itself as safe because of its compliance with current legislation and its correspondence with public opinion. The sign at the factory "Safety is key, it is up to you and me" illustrates this.
The slogan "Safe working is done together!" reduces safety to moral appeal and team spirit instead of effective risk management. Luhmann would miss a structural link between the company and the health and scientific systems. He would point at the organisation-specific legitimacy codes of reputation and trust.

"Safety is Key, it's up to You & Me –
Welcome at Eternit - Working safely is a team effort!"

The Public Prosecution Office in the Netherlands retrospectively sees previous decisions by Eternit as unlawful, despite the fact that asbestos production was legal before 1993. The legal code works through retroactive reinterpretation, especially when new distinctions such as criminal liability become available.

Eternit's decisions were guided by the economic system, which dictated cost-effective production. The asbestos risk was not operationalised as a constraint, but as an externality. It was known, but not economically disruptive, until external systems (legislation, public opinion) let the costs rise.

Since the 1960s, the health risks of asbestos were known within the scientific system. But scientific knowledge was not structurally linked to decision-making within companies like Eternit. Scientific evidence was selectively interpreted for compliance rather than prevention. The consequences of asbestosis and mesothelioma manifested decades later and did not influence the decision-making cycles of production planning and policy.
Thus, Eternit failed to develop sustainable structural connections between:
- Scientific evidence and organisational decision-making,
- Legal system and (more than minimal) compliance,
- Healthcare system and preventive anticipation of latent consequences.

If lawsuits or studies caused a brief surge of attention, this did not lead to a reconfiguration of the way the organisation observed itself. The digital sign and the safety slogans constitute ritualised safety communication. What is communicated is reassurance, and what is obscured is risk. And what is lost is the capacity for structural learning. Without operational translation across systems (law, science, economy, health), safety becomes a brand instead of a practice. Operational translation mechanisms, e.g. integrated risk protocols and participatory monitoring are needed to disrupt an organisation's economic programming before it is too late. The sign shows that 'Safety' can be useful for communication, branding, and compliance, but also quite irrelevant for actual protection.

Transition to chapter 8

We saw how safety management systems depend not only on formal structures but on trust, legitimacy, and even dissent. Power without coercion, trust without guarantees, and the careful introduction of friction are what keep communication flowing in high-risk environments. But what happens when rules themselves become obstacles to safe functioning? What happens when *following the rules* leads to dysfunction, and *breaking them* maintains system integrity? That's the paradox of the next chapter. Sometimes, systems survive not despite violations, but because of them. To understand this, we must explore what Luhmann called *brauchbare Illegalität* (useful illegality), the rule-breaking that keeps the rules alive.

Chapter 8 - Rule-Breaking as a system function?

Keywords: Useful Illegality, Systemic Legitimacy, Structural Coupling

Well I know I could be just another stranger
But to you I guess I'm just another fool
And you swear you like to live your live in danger
Then you hide behind a wall of silly rules
Nobody thinks the way I do
I guess that nobody dares
Your head's so full of things
So set your mind free of them
I'm breakin' the rules

Breaking All the Rules (Ozzy Osbourne)
Osbourne, Daisley, Wylde, Sinclair, Castillo, 1988

We often think of rule violations as failures. But what if, in complex systems, some violations are not only inevitable, but essential?

Useful illegality: When breaking rules keeps systems working

Formal organisations thrive on procedures: checklists, audits, safety plans, permits. These mechanisms provide structure and memory. They promise predictability in the face of complexity. But there's a catch. Systems often function best when their rules are selectively bent[67].

Luhmann recognised this tension as foundational. Organisations appear rational and orderly but rely on informal workarounds to get things done. In safety, this is especially true: the rulebook alone can't keep people safe. Instead, safety is maintained through judgment, collegiality, and selective deviance. That's not a flaw. It's how the system survives. Illegality in this context is adaptation instead of recklessness. It's the system adjusting where the procedure can't.

Frontline workers routinely make decisions that deviate from procedure but serve the system's deeper goals. A technician bypasses a protocol to prevent a more serious hazard. A labour inspector agrees to delay an audit to maintain future cooperation. These actions violate formal expectations but support systemic integrity. Luhmann formalised this idea as a systems necessity; a kind of internal flexibility masked by formal rigidity.

Luhmann called this *Brauchbare Illegalität*; that's German for useful illegality:
"*Organisations do not survive despite rule violations, but because of them*." – Luhmann[68]

If this sounds like cursing in church, here's the twist you were waiting for: When something goes wrong, these same deviations are often reframed as failures. What was once a smart workaround becomes an offence. Organisations protect their legitimacy by rewriting history. In other words, systems retroactively edit their own story to preserve coherence. Success becomes failure when the context changes. Cultural narratives and real-world cases show how rule-breaking heroes become scapegoats, or icons, depending on timing and interpretation. Many historic cases illustrate this, like this one:

Useful Illegality and the ambiguity of heroism
The case of Prince Friedrich von Homburg[69]

In a military engagement against the Swedish army, *Prince Friedrich von Homburg*[70], a young cavalry general in the service of the Great Elector of Brandenburg, defied a direct order. He led an unsanctioned attack that resulted in a decisive victory; one that, paradoxically, also became grounds for his court-martial.

Before the battle, the Great Elector had issued a clear command: the cavalry was to hold position and not engage until explicitly ordered. Prince Friedrich was distracted and did not register the command. He acted without knowing he was disobeying, which complicates the moral terrain. At the decisive moment, he ordered a charge, without command authority and against the rules of engagement. His boldness led to success. The enemy was put to flight. Yet instead of reward, the prince was arrested, tried, and sentenced to death for insubordination.

The prince's action illustrates a textbook case of what Luhmann called *useful illegality, a*n act that violates formal authority but achieves the system's broader goals. The prince was punished not because the outcome was bad, but because the means violated the system's procedural integrity. The system faced a dilemma: If it rewards the prince, it undermines command structure and encourages individual initiative over coordinated action. If it punishes him, it seems to disregard the victory and demoralise its most daring leaders. The Great Elector chose the latter: to defend the primacy of discipline over result. The prince was condemned, not despite his success, but because of it: his disobedience was dangerous precisely because it worked.

In a moment of reflection, the prince undergoes a transformation. Facing execution, he accepts the legitimacy of the sentence and the necessity of hierarchy in military life. The prince internalises the distinction between personal courage and systemic responsibility. Moved by this transformation and influenced by external pleas, the Elector ultimately withdraws the execution order, but only after the prince has submitted fully to the system's authority. The Elector's final act of pardon is staged as a ritual, a symbolic rebirth. The system, personified by the Elector, defends hierarchy, but only after witnessing that the prince has internalised its decision premises (i.e., the structured expectations guiding how decisions are made within the system). The lesson is that legitimacy matters more than innovation. The prince emerges not only victorious in battle but rehabilitated within the symbolic order. He's a hero for his final obedience.

This historical parable may seem distant from HSE management, but the logics are strikingly similar. Especially when accidents are avoided not by following the rules, but by knowing when to bend them.
Lessons for HSE Management:

- Not illegality, but *legitimacy* is the real issue. Systems tolerate rule-breaking when outcomes are favourable, but only if the breach can be retroactively framed within the system's values;
- Outcome ≠ Justification. Good results don't automatically validate the process. Systems often prioritise internal coherence over external success;
- Authority needs exceptions but also needs to punish them. This paradox is central to maintaining the credibility of rule-based systems;
- Recognition follows reintegration. The prince is not celebrated for defiance, but for ultimately recognising and submitting to systemic authority.

This case has significance to us in the 21st century: A frontline worker bypasses protocol to avert disaster, only to be reprimanded. Later, their action may be reframed as heroic, but only *after* the system absorbs the shock and reasserts its boundaries. In systems like aviation, healthcare, or military operations, useful illegality is often both a risk and a resource. Managing it requires balancing between rigidity and adaptation, between the letter of the rule and the spirit of resilience.

But what happens when the system can no longer recognise the value of informal adaptation. When it over-identifies with its procedures?

When formality obscures function

HSE management systems rely on formalisation to coordinate across complexity. But those same structures can suppress informal intelligence:

- Frontline knowledge is excluded if not in the proper format.
- Deviations are punished even when they prevent harm.
- Emotional realities such as fear, guilt and frustration are ignored in favour of procedural closure.

This creates the dangerous illusion that safety can be managed entirely through planning and reporting. But as any experienced safety professional knows, real work rarely matches what's on paper. It's in this space between paperwork and practice that useful illegality emerges. Not as sabotage, but as system repair. Deviations often trigger blame, not because they caused harm, but because they threaten the system's self-image.

Error management: The politics of blame

When systems fail, they don't always simply respond with learning. Instead, they often respond with symbolic correction:

- Committees are formed.
- Reports are rewritten.
- Responsibility is narrowed to individuals.

This preserves the appearance of rationality.

Luhmann showed[71] that symbolic correction helps organisations to manage contradiction. Deviations are not interpreted as symptoms of systemic stress, but as isolated errors. The system protects its legitimacy by framing failures as exceptions. This helps preserve internal stability, but often at the cost of learning.

Then, sanctions follow. These come in different forms. Formal sanctions follow rules. But many real sanctions are informal:

- A whistleblower is quietly transferred,
- A critical engineer is passed over for promotion, and
- A vocal critic is excluded from meetings.

These actions maintain internal peace and avoid overt disruption. They reaffirm control without naming the conflict.

In recent years, the language of psychological safety has tried to soften organisational climates. But Luhmann would warn that you can't change a system by changing how individuals feel. You have to change what communications are considered valid.

The trend of psychological safety
In Human Resource management and in HSE management too, *psychological safety* is a trending topic. Luhmann would stress that it's not doctors, nurses, or managers who fail to speak out or act; it's communication that succeeds or fails within the system. The individual may want to speak up. But unless the system is structured to register and respond to that input, it's filtered out. So, the issue is not whether individuals feel safe, but whether the communication system allows certain distinctions (e.g., problematic incident / normal incident) to be made and maintained.

Healthcare operates with its own functional code, something like healthy / ill or safe / unsafe. Ethics or whistleblowing introduces a different code, perhaps right / wrong or legal / illegal. Luhmann would say that cross-code communication (e.g., between ethics, law, and health systems) leads to misunderstanding, because each system operates by its own logic.
The concern with psychological safety or openness clashes with the operational code of the organisational system, which isn't designed to process dissent or moral critique effectively. The organisation (chemical factory, nuclear plant, hospital, etc.) is a self-referential system. It reproduces its structure through decision-making. Reports of malpractice threaten the system's identity, so they're often rejected, downplayed, or reframed.

The climate for expression is the result of how the system defines what counts as relevant communication. If reporting critical incidents isn't coupled to meaningful decisions, the system ignores it. The popular idea that an anonymous whistleblowing channel solves the problem is, to Luhmann, a simplification. It reduces complexity in a symbolic way but doesn't restructure communication pathways.
Change, in Luhmann's view, would mean embedding dissent and reflection into the formal structure of the organisation, as routine distinctions the system can process. The absence of open communication in healthcare is not a cultural failure but a structural one. If adverse event reporting is not meaningfully coupled to the decision-making processes of the system, communication about them will be filtered out, regardless of moral will. What is needed is not more freedom to speak, but new forms of organisational coupling that allow such communications to enter the system as decisions instead of disruptions.

Even when whistleblowers or the public speak out, the system may remain unmoved, unless the outrage can be translated into a form the system recognises.

Moral outrage, systemic blindness

In public safety controversies, like migrant worker exploitation or environmental lapses, moral outrage erupts. But outrage alone doesn't change systems. Why? Because systems don't see morality directly.
They process distinctions that are meaningful within their own logic:

- The economy sees price but not suffering,
- Law sees liability but not fairness, and
- Administration sees compliance but not lived conditions.

To influence systems, outrage must be translated into communicable codes: contracts, incentives, and legal risks. Otherwise, it remains invisible to the system. This is why reform often fails. Not for lack of passion, but for lack of translation between social outcry and systemic processing.

These translation failures become especially apparent when systems with different logics try to coordinate. Such as law and business.

Law and the Economy speak in different codes

The idea that 'safety pays' assumes that economic self-interest alone can drive better safety outcomes. But as Andrew Hopkins writes[72], this belief often fails in practice. Many serious events like near misses or illnesses with a long incubation time don't immediately translate into financial costs. Others, like compensation claims, are managed administratively without addressing real issues. This illustrates Luhmann's point that the economic system and the legal system operate with different codes. Where business sees safety as a cost-benefit calculation (profitable/unprofitable), the legal system sees it in terms of duty and culpability (legal/illegal). When these systems try to regulate one another, structural coupling is required; mechanisms that translate one code into terms the other can process.

Prosecutions, particularly those targeting individual managers, function as coupling points. They make legal consequences tangible within the economic system, determining what is real for decision-makers. But without sustained mechanisms to translate between these codes, safety gets lost in the noise of competing priorities. "There's no question about it," one manager told Hopkins. "Fear of prosecution was the motivator." Not cost or claims but law made itself visible.

Designing for failure without punishing learning

So how can safety systems evolve not by eliminating deviance, but by learning from it? How do we build safety management systems that learn from deviation instead of punishing it?

- Acknowledge informal work as part of the system;
- Create forums where ambiguity and discomfort can be discussed without retribution;
- Distinguish between violations of rules and failures of the system; and
- Allow for contradictions between performance and reality, between policy and practice.

These are structural couplings instead of merely soft reforms; mechanisms that let the system absorb difference without crisis. This doesn't mean we have to give up on formal rules. It means holding them lightly, using them as frameworks. The goal is not to purify the system, but to make it resilient; capable of holding contradiction without collapse.

Conclusion: Systems that tolerate contradiction
Luhmann's work teaches us a difficult but important lesson: contradiction is not a failure of the system. It's a condition of its operability. Formal rules give order. Informal adaptations give function. Together, they sustain the improbable normal.

The goal of safety work, then, is not to eliminate deviance, but to understand it. Not to close gaps between policy and practice, but to work intelligently within them.
Systems don't punish transgression but disruption. So, the real challenge is not rule-breaking itself, but how the system processes it. Does it treat deviation as betrayal, or as a signal for recalibration?

If safety is to be sustained, organisations must stop demanding purity and start designing for complexity. Because in reality, perfect systems don't exist. We need resilient ones.

Transition to chapter 9
We explored how organisations often rely on rule-bending to function effectively. But alongside procedural adaptations, organisations also engage in a different strategy to navigate contradiction. And that is, through moral appeals. When structural issues persist or formal coordination fails, the impulse to reach for values like care, courage, or responsibility grows stronger. Yet systems don't operate on morality; they operate on code.

What happens when safety is framed not as a coordination problem, but as a moral one? When cultural campaigns replace structural change? As we'll see in the next chapter, the limits of moral communication don't have to do much with empathy. Rather, they're signals of deeper systemic dissonance.

Chapter 9 – Morality as a safety strategy?!

Keywords: Functional Differentiation, Moral Communication, Structural Anomie

'Forward!' he cried from the rear / And the front rank died
And after all, we're only ordinary men
Us and Them (Pink Floyd)
Roger Waters, 1973

This chapter explores how safety, often framed as a moral imperative, operates more accurately as a function of interdependent systems. Drawing from systems theory, it argues that moral discourse, while well-intentioned, can obscure deeper contradictions between system logics. When values clash with structural incentives, tension arises. Understanding these tensions can help reframe safety as a structural coordination challenge, not a cultural or ethical failing.

In the face of complex risks and persistent breakdowns, HSE professionals often turn to the moral register. They hope values can do what procedures and structures have failed to achieve.

The trouble with good intentions
Safety professionals often lead with values:
- 'We care',
- 'Every life matters', and
- 'Zero Harm'.

Yet something still feels off. Why do well-intentioned programmes provoke resistance or even burnout? Why does "doing the right thing" feel so hard in organisational life? If you can relate to this tension, you're not alone. It's a systemic tension. When moral imperatives clash with operational realities, more than your personal frustration is the result. It's functional dissonance.

The French sociologist Émile Durkheim had a word for this: *anomie.* This refers to a condition of normlessness, not the absence of norms, but the presence of incompatible or disintegrated ones. In organisational life, this can manifest as value dissonance, where formal messages contradict lived reality, leading to confusion, disengagement, or deviance. In safety, this emerges when slogans like 'stop the job' clash with the quiet pressure to stay quiet or hit targets. Not from a lack of norms, but from too many contradictory ones:

- 'Work as imagined' vs. 'work as done'
- KPIs that discourage reporting, and
- Safety rhetoric vs. production incentives.

We often label these as cultural problems, but they are symptoms of systemic contradiction. The dissonance becomes especially tangible when organisational reforms focus on messaging but leave underlying incentives untouched.

When structure outpaces meaning

Durkheim showed how societies fragment when regulation fails to keep up with expectations[73]. Luhmann's student Stefan Kühl adds that efforts to 'change culture' often fail not due to resistance, but because leaders ignore the informal expectations that already govern behaviour[74].

If management changes slogans but not systems, ambiguity sets in. People adapt, sometimes in deviant but entirely rational ways. They don't reject any values but adapt to contradictory demands that the formal system refuses to reconcile. As Michael Power writes, risk management organises what can't be organised[75]. Control becomes ritual, and unresolved tensions persist. For example: if collaboration is praised but only competitive individuals are promoted, what behaviour actually survives? Culture, Kühl argues[76], is not a canvas to repaint with workshops or posters. It's formed by repetition, contradiction, and what's left unsaid. Again, these are not merely theoretical contradictions. They manifest every day in how safety is managed, measured, and misunderstood.

Visible anomie in safety

Consider these contradictions that surface daily in HSE management:

- Hazard reporting systems require detailed input but reward speed over completeness
- 'Stop the job' messages clash with fear of sanctions, and
- Incident categories obscure context rather than clarify it.

We can label these as failures of culture, but then we miss that they are symptoms of structural anomie where formal rules and informal expectations drift apart. To understand why moral messaging struggles in complex organisations, we need to look at how modern society is structured around specialised functions instead of shared values.

From values to systems: Functional differentiation
Luhmann observed that modern society no longer revolves around shared morality, but around functionally differentiated subsystems[77]. Each has its own code, its own logic of what counts as relevant. These codes don't reflect right or wrong, but operational necessity. This makes cross-system communication fragile, especially when one system tries to moralise another.

Subsystem	Code	Example
Law	Legal/Illegal	Was the action lawful?
Economy	Profit/Loss	Can we afford this control?
Politics	Power/Powerless	What position does this support?
Medicine	Healthy/Sick	Was the person fit to work?
Media	Information/non-information	Will this attract attention?

These codes are the reality within each system. However, when their logic clashes, we often mistake systemic dissonance for moral failure:
Unsafe ≠ Illegal.
Bad ≠ Unprofitable.
False ≠ Uninformative.

These mismatches aren't simply ethical failures. They're *communication failures between systems with incompatible definitions of relevance*. We can accuse managers, politicians, or scientists of not caring about safety, but *their systems construct what is relevant differently*.

When the structural coupling between subsystems weakens, they start talking past each other:
- Politics provides visibility instead of governance.
- Media amplifies moral outrage instead of promoting understanding.
- Law is seen as too slow to be useful.
- Science is ignored in favour of more resonant stories.
- Economics becomes symbolic, not strategic.

This is what Luhmann would call code fragmentation. Every system speaks, but no system hears the same language.
For the media in particular, this fragmentation is structural. As Luhmann puts it, the media provide a background reality. They provide a dynamic stream of what is "known for the sake of being known." The media do this through selection criteria such as surprise, norm violation, moral outrage, and personalisation.

These selection criteria make news seem truthful, but inevitably biased. So, when HSE news fails to get through, it's often because it's coded as noninformation. It does not meet the media threshold for novelty or conflict. In other words, its reality is not ignored but filtered out.

Moral messages become most visible when systems can't enforce coupling. Safety campaigns, for instance, often reveal where functional coupling has failed.

When posters plead road users to be more careful

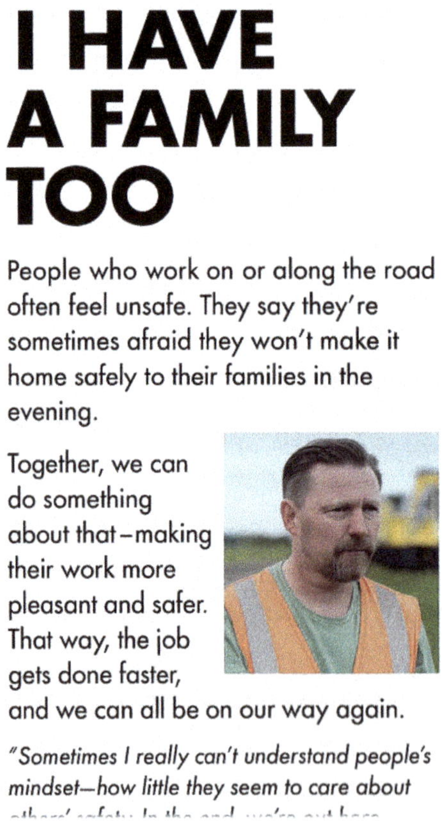

You might have come across a campaign like this one[78]. It features posters of construction workers asking drivers to slow down, follow instructions, and show empathy; "I have a family too." These are powerful emotional messages. But from

Luhmann's perspective, they reveal more about systemic failure than about personal care. When messages from one system (e.g. safety policy) are ignored by others (e.g. drivers responding to time pressure or economic logic), campaigns resort to moral communication: pleas, guilt, and empathy. Luhmann would argue: Moral appeals increase when system couplings fail.

Mind you, roads themselves communicate values: a fast design, with wide lanes and no crossings suggest speed is normal[79]. When infrastructure invites fast driving, but signs tell drivers to slow down and be careful, the contradiction falls on the shoulders of individuals, especially the most vulnerable (e.g. road workers). From this perspective, moral messages like "Drive safely for us" serve as compensatory rituals in a system that has failed to structurally line up its priorities. Emotional labour replaces legal enforcement. In such moments, morality is used to plug the gap between design and reality, in an attempt to restore order through sentiment rather than structure. Safety is framed as personal decency instead of a design function.

In short:
- Moral appeals rise where functional translation fails;
- Emotional messaging often compensates for design contradictions;
- When road design favours speed, safety campaigns become symbolic; and
- Anomie results not from a lack of norms, but from conflicting system logics.

Rather than trying to fix culture or to raise awareness, ethical safety work might ask: *Which systems aren't listening, and how can their codes be translated?* Safety is a theme or semantic domain that travels across systems that don't have a unified code. Each system processes safety in its own operationally closed way.
As these contradictions accumulate, we often retreat to the language of *culture*. But this too has limits, especially when it replaces systemic diagnosis with vague aspirations.

Culture talk has its limits

In HSE, we often talk about culture, be it "safety culture" or organisational culture. Luhmann's student Stefan Kühl warns that culture often becomes a stand-in for the unexplained; a 'terminological vacuum cleaner'. It's used for everything we can't explain away: "*The culture's not proactive*". Culture becomes a narrative container large enough to hold contradiction, but too vague to resolve it.

But if communication structures are not lined up, no amount of values talk or mission statements can compensate. Culture doesn't fail because of bad intentions or because people are not socialised with safety as a value. It fails because structure contradicts meaning. The solution isn't to abandon values, but to recognise where they fail to travel across system boundaries.

So how should we respond? Not by doubling down on moral appeals, but by asking:

- What 'good/bad' distinction is in play?
- Which system's logic is being used?
- Are we moralising a structural contradiction?

Ethics, here, means observing how moral communication functions instead of just what it says. One popular attempt to operationalise values is the Safety Culture Ladder. But like many tools, it reflects what systems can measure, not necessarily what matters.

The Safety Culture Ladder: Useful, but incomplete

Yes, the Safety Culture Ladder it tries to 'measure' culture. But:

- It misses fear, trust, and informal norms
- It confuses behaviour with belief, and
- It ignores how systems interpret the same behaviour differently.

As a result, it creates the illusion of insight while leaving structural contradictions untouched. My advice: Use it (it's mandatory in a lot of sectors after all), but combine it with ethnography, interviews, and humble listening.

So, Luhmann wrote that even assumptions are shaped by system codes. A CFO and a safety officer may share values but operate under different logics: cost vs. risk. Both are valid, within their system. If we take Luhmann seriously, the task isn't to line up people with culture, but to structurally couple systems with one another.

From culture change to system coupling

Instead of trying to "Fix the culture," we can ask:

- Which systems are interacting?
- Where do their codes conflict?
- What interface can bridge the difference?

In system terms, these are *coupling mechanisms*; points of translation between different operational logics. If incident reports are ignored, perhaps it's not apathy, but that they're written in safety logic, not financial bottom-line, to name just one relevant code.

This flips the usual script: where we see a lack of values, we might instead find a lack of systemic coupling. Moral appeals are often used where structural redesign is needed. So instead of asking "Why don't they care?", we should ask "How is their system structured to hear?"

One more time: When moral discourse escalates, ask:

- What codes are clashing?
- What design changes could translate between them?
- Remember: Ethical safety work listens sharper than it shouts.

In this view, ethics is not a louder voice, but a better ear. It seeks the patterns beneath the values and asks: what kind of listening does this system enable?

Transition to chapter 10

We saw how moral appeals emerge where systems fail to coordinate. But even when morality fades and systems return to their functional codes, problems remain. Safety is rarely derailed by bad intentions or values; more often safety is created, and constrained, by decision programmes. These programmes define what counts as relevant, measurable, and fundable.

Chapter 10 – How goals legitimise but rarely guide action

Keywords: Decision Programmes, Operationalisation, Goal Paradox

Welcome my son, welcome to the machine
What did you dream?
It's all right, we told you what to dream
Welcome to the machine (Pink Floyd)
Roger Waters, 1975

While the previous chapter showed how moral appeals often misfire in functionally differentiated systems, this chapter explores a different mechanism of coordination: decision-making. If values can't always guide action, decisions at least claim to. But in Luhmann's theory, even decisions don't drive behaviour as directly as we think. They organise uncertainty but rarely resolve it. We need to understand why goals, however clear or noble, often serve more as retrospective justifications than as operational compasses.

Decisions as the basic unit of organisation
Modern organisations are not primarily designed to act, but to decide. According to Luhmann, organisations consist of decisions that lead to further decisions, creating a *recursive structure*[80]. In HSE management, this means every rule, form, or checklist is a scaffold for future decisions.

In Luhmann's systems theory, a decision is the selection among alternatives, which then re-enters the system as a premise for future choices. Decision-making doesn't eliminate uncertainty, of course; it stabilises it but always generates new uncertainties in return. HSE management illustrates this well through its ever-expanding decision-support systems and change management protocols. To understand how decisions function in organisations, we need to unpack how they are structured. Luhmann introduced the idea of decision programmes; templates that determine how decisions can be made, justified, and replicated. They are *scaffolds of selection*.

Decision programmes: Purpose, Condition, Action
Luhmann wrote[81] that goals are not causal drivers but legitimising narratives, often formed after the fact to provide coherence to decisions. Present decisions reference past ones, while their future impact remains unpredictable. This structure invites hindsight bias into learning practices: after an incident, risk logs retroactively impose order on what was fundamentally uncertain.

Zero Harm: A goal or a simplification?
The goal of 'Zero Harm' is a prime example. Zero Harm is often treated as a moral imperative, but in systems terms, it's better understood as a symbolic goal. It simplifies reality into a singular direction, which allows systems to act without consensus on deeper meaning. It's not that the goal is insincere, but that its role is functional instead of motivational. In practice, Zero Harm becomes a heuristic. It makes safety decidable, allowing action without full clarity. Its function lies not in being achievable, but in guiding attention and coordinating behaviour under uncertainty.

Once an abstract goal like Zero Harm is declared, it requires translation. This translation process turns the broad commitment into discrete, reportable actions. But this transformation changes the goal's nature from ethical direction to procedural output.

Operationalisation and Algorithmisation
To enact abstract goals like Zero Harm, organisations translate them into measurable actions:

- Operationalisation: e.g., "Install 300 safety barriers," or "Hold a daily toolbox meeting."
- Algorithmisation: e.g., "If risk > $1x10^{-4}$, then mitigate," using risk matrices or compliance software.

These translations distribute responsibility and make performance trackable. Yet, they often narrow the meaning of safety to what is easily measurable. As a result, compliance can replace vigilance.

Optimisation and its limits

The drive to optimise is borrowed from economics, where decisions are framed as rational calculations for the best outcome. But in complex systems, clearly defined goals are rare. Optimisation can obscure value conflicts and mask the partial, bounded nature of real decisions.
Luhmann saw this and proposed alternatives like satisficing[82] (solutions that are good enough) and suboptimisation (partial improvements within constraints). He warned against conflating goals, motivations, and systemic functions. In organisations, people are often motivated by salary or habit instead of by overarching goals. The paradox is that the more a system tries to optimise for safety, the more it risks flattening safety into what is measurable, instead of what is meaningful. The goal that once justified action becomes a constraint on reflection.

This paradox is illustrated in attempts to exclude safety from market dynamics altogether. Well-intentioned principles can backfire if they misunderstand the functional codes of other systems, particularly the economy.

"Let there be no competition on safety!"

A government organisation had the principle of "No competition on safety". The intention was that working safely is non-negotiable. Despite this good intention, the principle led to unintended negative consequences, as contractors sought the boundaries of working safely.

Luhmann wrote that in the economic system, prices are the medium through which decisions are made and communicated. When safety is excluded from pricing, we effectively remove it from the communication system of the economy. The implication of this is that the economic system (here: contractors) can't properly process safety as a meaningful element unless it's monetarily quantified. Without a price, the costs of working safely are not compensated and a client certainly does not have to expect new innovations regarding working safely.

By removing safety from competition and pricing, safety becomes invisible to the decision-making of both the contracting authority and the bidder. The economic system is not designed to integrate non-priced expectations, and it's by default focused on minimising costs. This often comes at the expense of non-priced values such as working safely. The unintended consequence is that "No competition on safety!", intended as universal compliance with safety standards, becomes in practice unfunded compliance. This leads to underperformance.

Where public administration operates on the basis of normative agreements (e.g. 'safety first for all'), markets operate on the basis of price signals. Trying to impose the former on the latter without translation, i.e. cost sharing, causes friction. The administrative fiction that "working safely is the norm" removes the mechanisms (price, audit, trade-off analysis) that actually guarantee that safety is achieved in complex, cost-driven projects. Luhmann would say that structural coupling between public administration and economy is necessary for mutual influence. Not pricing safety prevents this coupling. The administration expects safety; the market sees no price signal; safety is eliminated.

To restore the functional coupling between administrative expectations and economic activities:
- Specify the costs of working safely. Do this not to enable competition on safety, but to ensure its reality.
- Check the presence of safety in bids, not just as a yes/no checkbox, but as an operational plan linked to resources.

Types of control in organisations
Luhmann identified three types of control:
1. *Crisis Control* re-examines the usefulness of entire programmes during crises.
2. *Indicator Control* questions whether indicators chosen (e.g., LTIF) actually capture programme performance.
3. *Comparative Control* compares expected and actual outcomes, not primarily to punish but to enable learning and adaptation.

Each of Luhmann's control types reveals a different layer of how organisations maintain their own observability. But HSE management systems often collapse these forms into the simplest one: checklist completion. Reflexivity, true second-order observation, is often lost.

The *identity function* of safety goals deserves attention. Beyond management, goals like Zero Harm become performative symbols. They communicate organisational virtue, even when they distort internal feedback.

Zero Harm as symbol and risk
Zero Harm also acts as an identity marker: "*We care about safety!*" But this can have perverse effects:
- Underreporting to protect the goal,
- Redefining incidents to fit the narrative, and
- Focusing on metrics over meaning.

Luhmann would urge us to ask: What does our pursuit of Zero Harm say about how we observe safety? When a goal turns sacred, it quickly stops being useful. Goals must remain open to scrutiny.

Drawing on Luhmann, we can see safety goals as:
1. Communicative simplifications that structure uncertainty;
2. Narratives that semantically legitimise decisions after the fact;
3. Standards that make safety decidable;
4. Paradoxical anchors; the more unattainable the goal, the more it legitimises action.

Goals don't need to be fully met, but they need to enable structured reflection and justify action. In this sense, goals are less about setting direction and more about maintaining operability. They anchor the system, not because they are true or reachable, but because they reduce the ambiguity of what counts as action.

Managing, not eliminating, uncertainty
Organisations absorb complexity, but they don't solve it. Systems use[83]:
- Abstraction, when they turn complexity into simplified categories like risk or compliance;
- Delegation, when they transfer responsibility to tools and processes;
- Temporising, when they defer difficult decisions until conditions change.

These methods make uncertainty actionable, even if not fully resolved. What we find, then, is that the utility of goals lies more in enabling decisions than in determining their content. This reframing challenges conventional management logics that treat goals as drivers. In complex systems, goals are functions of communication. They organise the possibility of movement instead of its destination.

Conclusion: The machine metaphor revisited
Organisations are not machines for making perfect decisions. At best, they are machines for *maintaining the capacity to decide*. Formal structures don't eliminate uncertainty but they make non-decision look like defective processing.

Transition to chapter 11
If safety goals like 'Zero Harm' serve more to legitimise decisions than to guide them, the next question becomes: Who is expected to make those decisions? In practice, that burden often falls on leaders, those tasked with steering organisations through complexity, contradiction, and constant uncertainty. Leadership, like goal setting, is often framed as more transparent and authoritative than it truly is. In structurally

complex and functionally differentiated systems, the leader can't simply see the problem and fix it. Observation itself is selective, contingent, and influenced by the system one tries to guide. Let's explore what leadership looks like when clarity is impossible, control is limited, and humility becomes a strength rather than a weakness.

Chapter 11 – Leadership in structurally opaque systems

Keywords: Second-Order Observation, Structural Coupling, Epistemic Humility

You may ask yourself / How do I work this?
Once in a Lifetime (Talking Heads)
Brian Eno, 1980

Leadership in safety is often imagined as a matter of clear guidance and firm oversight. But what happens when oversight is misread. Clarity can become intrusion. The true story that follows is a parable about how influence is never just about intention, but also about how the message is processed.

The safety manager and the painted window
A safety professional, newly trained in influencing techniques, observes construction workers on scaffolding without fall protection. From his office window, he tackles the problem head-on by clearly formulating the standards. The intention is to communicate clearly for compliance. The next morning, at the start of his shift, he sees that his office window has been painted white, completely blocking the view of the scaffolding...

The safety message, intended as normative clarity, is interpreted by the workers as a threat to autonomy and/or trust. This illustrates an important point in Luhmann's systems theory: messages don't carry fixed meanings. What matters is not *what* is said, but *how it becomes meaningful within the system's logic*. The painted window symbolises a clear boundary that is being drawn. In complex systems, even what is intended as help for working safely can be read as one-sided supervision. Meaning arises within systems from the way messages are processed. In safety management, too, influence begins where control ends.

From this anecdote, we zoom out. Leadership is a matter of understanding how signals are selected, filtered, and repurposed by the system itself.

The illusion of transparent leadership

There is a common belief that leaders should be all-seeing, all-knowing figures capable of making fully informed decisions. This expectation is comforting, and fictional. In reality, leaders operate within highly complex, functionally differentiated systems. Niklas Luhmann reminds us that systems are operationally closed: they don't respond directly to external inputs, but rather to internal structures and distinctions. Leaders don't stand outside the organisation observing it objectively; they are part of the system they try to steer. Rather than seeing leadership as a heroic act of will, we see it here as a recursive act of observation: observing not just the organisation, but how the organisation observes itself.

Leadership in Luhmann's terms is less about commanding from above and more about observing how the system observes itself. Leaders must understand the organisation's internal filters: its blind spots, habitual exclusions, and preferred categories of meaning. The distinction between system and environment isn't a true representation of the world, but a constructed way to manage complexity.

Now, one of the most underappreciated resources leaders manage is not authority or information, but time. Decisions can't solve uncertainty, so, they stretch it forward.

Reflexivity and the temporalisation of complexity

In organisations, decisions do more than resolve questions. They create the conditions for future decisions. This recursive structure introduces uncertainty through time. Leadership is about managing time as much as information. This means good leadership is less about predicting outcomes and more about enabling resilient futures, narratives and structures that remain adaptive over time. Leaders must craft plausible narratives that help the system orient toward the future, without pretending to predict it.

But even the best narratives can't eliminate one of the most basic features of modern systems: opacity. Leaders must work within a horizon they can't fully see.

Structural opacity as a necessary limitation

The challenge of leadership is not simply a lack of tools or data. It's structural, because systems can only observe what fits their observational framework. Leadership, then, requires not more data, but better awareness of what data one's system is blind to. Clarity isn't achieved by seeing more, but *by understanding what remains unseeable*. This structural blindness becomes especially visible when systems must coordinate across different domains. A prime example is when legal and scientific logics collide in the aftermath of failure.

Legal expectations vs. scientific uncertainty
This becomes especially clear in high-stakes domains like safety. Consider the structural tension between law and science:
- Law operates in binary terms: legal / illegal;
- Science works with probabilistic distinctions: true / untrue.

Law demands decisive outcomes: causality, blame, and accountability. Science, by contrast, often produces *open-ended models* and *conditional knowledge*. When these systems clash in the aftermath of accidents, the result can be systemic misunderstanding. Neither system is wrong, but each processes reality through a different operational logic. Leadership must mediate these mismatches without pretending they can be fully harmonised. In real events, like the Ketel Bridge tragedy, we see how functional codes can diverge with tragic consequences.

Ketel Bridge in Motorway A6 in the Netherlands[84]

> In the Netherlands, a tragic accident occurred at the Ketel Bridge on Highway A6. A driver missed the first barrier coming down, reversed when the second one came down, and fell into the water as the bridge rose. The Public Prosecutor blamed the bridge operator, arguing the accident should have been prevented. The operator, however, physically could not see that section from the control booth.
>
> A critical newspaper column[85] highlighted this judicial blind spot: assuming that "what should have been seen" is the same as "what could have been seen." The author, a Human Factors Specialist, cited a similar case involving a truck driver who was convicted despite never having had visual access to a motorcyclist hidden by terrain. Only a Human Factors expert's reconstruction mitigated the sentence. The law demanded certainty; the science offered only probability. The disconnect is systemic.

Legal and perceptual systems didn't line up in this case. Luhmann would call it a failure of structural coupling: two systems (law and science) failing to translate meaning between their internal logics.

Epistemic humility in leadership

Leaders and judges often overestimate their ability to see clearly. They ignore the *epistemic constraints* of their own system. In these moments, leadership can't assert truth from above. It must work from within limited perspectives. This is where epistemic humility becomes strategic. Leadership today demands *epistemic humility*. It's defined as *the recognition that all decisions are made through the limited perspectives of one's system*. Clarity is not achieved through heroic control, but through iterative learning and sensitivity to weak signals. Luhmann argues that organisations steer through their self-descriptions: "We are agile," "We are learning," and so forth. These narratives help guide action, but they also conceal as much as they reveal. Leaders must therefore treat organisational narratives as both tools and traps, useful for coordination, but dangerous if mistaken for complete comprehension. This points to a sobering, but empowering view of leadership: not as omniscience, but as guided sense-making within structural constraints.

Conclusion
Leadership in complex systems is not about knowing everything. It's about steering responsibly in conditions of permanent partial visibility. The task is not to eliminate opacity, but to work within it; to accept that *guidance*, not control, is the work of leadership. The task is not to master the system, but to participate in its reflexivity. To help the organisation see how it sees, and act with care despite what it can't know. And to remain reflexive about the stories we tell ourselves about who we are and what we see. You can't steer what you can't observe. And you can't observe without selecting and thereby excluding.

Transition to chapter 12
If leadership in complex systems means steering amid uncertainty and structural opacity, then what exactly are we seeing when we observe safety? We saw that leaders operate within blind spots caused by their own systems. But safety itself is not an objective condition to be discovered. It's a distinction created through observation. What counts as 'error', 'risk', or 'compliance' depends on how the system defines and processes reality. To lead or manage safety effectively, we must not only observe events, but we must observe how we observe. This is the move from first order to second-order observation.

Chapter 12 – How safety constructs its own risks

Keywords: Second-Order Observation, Interface Design, Constructivist Safety

Looking down on empty streets, all she can see
Are the dreams all made solid, are the dreams made real
Pulling out the paper from the drawer marked 'secret'
Mercy Street
Peter Gabriel, 1986

Most safety conversations focus on surface events, like accidents, violations, and causes. But what if these are just the outputs of a deeper logic? Before we can manage risk in a different way, we need to ask: how is risk even made visible in the first place?

Observing the observer
Safety practice often stops at first-order observation: what went wrong, who erred, what rule was broken. But Luhmann[86] and his student Dirk Baecker[87] go deeper and ask: how is observation itself structured?

- Who defines what counts as 'safe'?
- What remains unobserved because of the lens we use?
- What does it mean to observe the observer?

Seems philosophical, right? But it has practical consequences. We change from managing behaviour to questioning the filters through which behaviour is interpreted. From assuming risk is objective, we start seeing it as dependent on the system doing the observing.

The A7 Crash and the social media assumption
Take a conversation I overheard about a decade ago between a road inspector and a traffic management consultant: *"Don't bother investigating the crash on Highway A7 this morning. I'm positive the driver who hit the barrier was on social media."* Notice what happened here: before any evidence was gathered, the event was already framed through the familiar lens of *distracted driving*. The assumption made the crash visible as 'human error', while excluding other possible contributing factors (road design, signage, barrier placement, vehicle condition). This illustrates how risk is never simply observed, but constructed through distinctions that foreground some explanations and blind us to others.

Communication makes safety visible (and invisible). Luhmann saw communication as the creation of form; every selection includes a distinction and a blind spot. Our safety dashboards, reports, and safety alerts create structured redundancy. What we label as "known risks" are selections that hide surprises. Information, then, is not what's communicated, but *the difference that makes a difference*. When we label something unsafe or 'human error', we assume we're naming objective facts. But Luhmann shows that what we call reality is influenced by the distinctions we use to describe it.

Constructivism in safety

Most safety models treat events and errors as objective realities waiting to be identified. But from Luhmann's constructivist view, 'human error' is not a fact but a distinction, a way of coding behaviour within a system's logic. The label 'Human error' is the result of a system observing a deviation from its expectations. This means error isn't just what someone did, but how the system chooses to frame what was done. And that framing tells us more about the system than about the person.

Therefore, we must ask:

- Who defined this as an error?
- Was it framed as deviation, or as adaptation?
- How is the human being constructed in this narrative: hero, scapegoat, noise, redundancy?

"*The human being is not a category that systems observe from outside. It is constructed within communication*." - Luhmann[88]

Safety professionals, too, are not neutral observers; they are part of the system's observation logic. This brings us to a crucial element often overlooked in safety: interfaces. It's where systems meet humans.

Interfaces between people and systems

Interfaces like checklists, handovers, or control panels are often seen as neutral conduits. But Baecker, following Luhmann, reframes them as filters, selective surfaces between otherwise incompatible systems. What gets communicated depends on what fits the interface logic. Just like a form with pre-set categories influences the answers it receives, every safety interface selects what counts as visible, and what disappears in silence. What doesn't fit is filtered out, unseen, and unreacted to. We must invite reflection: What do our interfaces select for? And what gets systematically excluded?

To move beyond reactive safety management, we need tools that examine not just what went wrong, but *how the system framed what could go wrong*. These are second-order tools, designed to reveal the assumptions behind the analysis.

Deciding how to observe
Observation always involves distinction-making: safe/unsafe, compliant/noncompliant, cause/consequence.
Second-order safety tools (e.g., learning teams) must focus not just on what happened, but on how the situation was framed, too.

Here are some questions that can be used to find out how frames were used:
- What assumptions guided the decision-making?
- Which alternatives were not even on the radar?
- What language was used to describe the actor: expert, violator, or 'human factor'?

These labels define the boundaries of action and accountability. The same behaviour can be read as innovation or insubordination, depending on the frame.

Another challenge lies in *time*. Communication happens in moments, but systems freeze those moments into categories that can become outdated, misleading, or even dangerous.

Temporal blindness and complexity
Communication is time-bound; it disappears as it happens. The documentation in our safety management systems freeze a fleeting moment, making it seem stable. Categories like 'human error' persist long past their usefulness. Yet the system has moved on: People adapt, and categories fossilise.

When seatbelts hide other risks
Think of incident reports that cite 'failure to wear seatbelt' as the root cause of injuries, even years after the nature of the work has changed. New patterns of risk go unnoticed because they don't fit the old labels. For example, service trucks that once had two people on board are now staffed by a single driver who must manually monitor and update three different portable information systems while driving. In this setting, the work often depends on hopping on and off quickly, so forgetting the seatbelt is almost built into the task. The hazard of cognitive overload and distraction is hidden by the official records that keep pointing to seatbelts.

So, we must continually revisit the distinctions we use:
- Are they still meaningful?
- What behaviours are emerging that don't fit?

Risks are dynamic. As work changes, so must our ways of seeing it. Otherwise, we're protecting against yesterday's dangers while missing today's signals.

Meta-methodological reflection: The limits of control
Formal systems simplify reality by design, but what gets simplified becomes normalised, and what gets normalised becomes invisible. Even algorithms, by reducing uncertainty, produce new blind spots. Therefore, reflexivity is not a luxury in safety, but a necessity. Now, this abstract theory comes alive when we examine real cases. The next example shows how a simple interface decision can produce systemic misunderstanding.

The double mouse and the invisible design
In September 2018, a bridge operator in Groningen, the Netherlands, accidentally closed a bridge too early, causing a ship to collide with it. The operator was controlling two bridges using nearly identical computer interfaces, each with its own mouse. In the critical moment, he used the wrong mouse. At first glance, this appears to be 'human error'. But a second-order analysis asks: how was the system structured such that this error became likely?

The control setup lacked clear visual or tactile differences between interfaces. There were no safeguards: no confirmation prompts, no labels, no checks. The system assumed the operator knew which bridge each mouse controlled. This was a structural flaw. The system was unable to recognise its own fragility. And in the absence of that recognition, it placed the burden of failure on the individual.
A court ruling held the operator legally responsible under Article 5 of the Dutch Road Traffic Act. But an ergonomics expert criticised the decision[89]: "The judge should take a course in ergonomics—and empathy." The ruling relied too heavily on the 'human error' label, ignoring the systemic design flaws that enabled the mistake.
This case reminds us that what seems like 'human error' is often the residue of unexamined design assumptions. The interface didn't fail because the operator was careless, but because the system never questioned itself.

What can we learn?

- Interfaces must reflect and test their own assumptions. Errors often reveal structural blind spots, not individual failings, and
- Reflexivity must be built into design (e.g., "Are you sure you want to close Bridge A?").

This case also illustrates what Luhmann called *functional differentiation*: law, science, and organisation viewed the event through different lenses:

- Law: Was it legal?
- Science: Was the design cognitively sound?
- Organisation: Was the risk managed?

These subsystems failed to connect. The legal judgment came before an ergonomic understanding. Without *structural coupling* (interfaces between these subsystems) we end up punishing errors we barely understand.
As Luhmann said, "Miscommunication is the norm." In safety, the challenge is not to eliminate these differences, but to design systems that can see, question, and adapt to them.

If we want more resilient systems, we need more reflexive observers. That means treating observation itself as a safety-critical activity.

Pluralistic and reflexive HSE practice
To improve HSE, we must go beyond objectivity, beyond error counting, beyond the illusion of neutrality.

We must reflect on:

- How the observer is constructed (e.g., 'expert witness', 'complacent worker');
- How the system creates roles that pre-shape what people can say or see; and
- How our distinctions guide, constrain, or enable action.

Reflexive tools for safety professionals

- What distinctions do your reports rely on?
- Where is silence encoded?
- Who defines what counts as 'evidence'?
- Is 'human error' a cause, or an outcome of system observation?

These are day-to-day entry points for changing how we document, investigate, and learn. *Reflexivity is a survival strategy in complexity.*

Conclusion: Reframing observation as responsibility
Learning in HSE management requires asking not just what happened, but how we came to see it that way.
And maybe what we keep failing to see. True safety work begins not with control, but with curiosity; with asking how our own ways of seeing may be the very thing that needs to change.

Transition to chapter 13
We have uncovered how safety is constructed, filtered, and framed by the systems that claim to measure and manage it. But how do we design for what we can't fully know? If observation is always partial, and risk is always filtered, then certainty becomes structurally impossible. Welcome to the terrain of 'not-knowing'! Our challenge is not to *control* uncertainty, but to *organise it meaningfully*.

Chapter 13 - Designing for not-knowing

Keywords: Reflexivity, Temporising, Procedural Confidence

Well, I see trouble at every turn
I've got so many lessons to learn
What am I doing wrong? I don't know
I Don't Know
Paul McCartney, 2018

Having seen how observation influences what HSE professionals perceive as real, we now turn to the structural issue: Certainty is unattainable. This chapter explores the uncomfortable but vital task of working *with* instead of *against* uncertainty.

Working without guarantees
What does it mean to practice safety in systems that can't be controlled, fully understood, or even clearly defined? Safety professionals are often asked to ensure outcomes in environments where even what counts as safe is a moving target. Now this is a structural challenge. Luhmann's makes clear: in modern, functionally differentiated society, the idea of certainty is itself a comforting illusion. In this view, safety is not about eliminating risk but about managing communication under conditions of limited knowledge. Instead of control, we seek coherence; instead of certainty, we seek coordination.

"*One cannot sufficiently know the future; not even the future that one brings about through one's own decisions*" — Luhmann[90]

Let's reflect on how safety work can be practiced when final solutions are out of reach and uncertainty is the basic condition of modern systems. To deal with this reality, we must stop imagining organisations as machines that just need better instructions. Instead, we need to understand how meaning is constructed through what systems choose to pay attention to, and what they ignore.

The limits of control and the possibilities of communication
Luhmann's idea is simple but radical: systems reduce complexity by producing meaning through communication, not by eliminating uncertainty[91]. We might think that the default

mode of system functioning is control, but in reality, it's *selective blindness*. To act at all, organisations must ignore much of what could matter. The challenge is not to see everything risky – what we might think 'chronic unease' means[92] -, but to become aware of how we see and what we don't. Luhmann argues that *opacity is a structural necessity*.

"*Organisations can only function by defining what does not need to be known; through decision premises, routines, and culture – so that not everything must be decided or communicated at every moment*." - Luhmann[93]

Organisations can only function if they define what need not be known. Total transparency would paralyse decision-making. This doesn't mean we should give up on trying to comprehend. We must design our systems to work responsibly within partial visibility. Good safety work is strategically aware of its own blind spots. Therefore, effective HSE management doesn't chase full visibility. It carefully frames what can remain unknown. This means changing our focus from eliminating failure to cultivating interdependence among roles and routines. Luhmann's abstract ideas have very real consequences. The Deepwater Horizon disaster can be reinterpreted as a breakdown of reflective safety design under pressure.

Macondo: A tragedy of temporary blindness

The Macondo oil spill off the southern coast of the United States was caused by an explosion following a blowout on the Deepwater Horizon semisubmersible platform. The blowout is often interpreted as a failure of engineering or individual judgment. But let's look at how systems managed uncertainty[94].

Every safety barrier (the well bottom cementing, the integrity test, the blowout preventer) was based on the unconfirmed assumption that previous steps had worked. The organisation had enough procedures, but did not reflect on its own assumptions when uncertainty arose.

Instead of creating space for reviewing decisions, the process design compressed time, eliminated pauses, and prioritised cost and completion. Procedural steps were followed but not re-examined. Observations became confirmations. Time to reflect was delegated. What failed was not only the engineering, but also the organisation's ability to doubt itself. In complex systems, the lack of a pause is a design flaw. Systems need spaces for second-order observation; moments to reflect on how assumptions are formed and carried forward.

The Deepwater Horizon disaster reminds us that in complex systems, safety comes not from thicker manuals or smarter tools, but from designing for not knowing. That means making time not just for reaction, but also for pause, doubt, and second-line observation.

It means recognising that trust in procedure should never replace curiosity about context.

This is what Luhmann called procedural trust gone too far: trust in form overwhelms awareness of function. Safety procedures were not ignored, but they became symbolic rituals rather than adaptive structures.

Deepwater Horizon is not a story about deviance, but a warning about how systems can end in disaster when they follow their own logic too faithfully, without recognising how that logic limits their vision.

If full control is not possible, what strategies remain? Luhmann doesn't leave us empty-handed. He identifies how systems stabilise complexity. Not by knowing more, but by abstracting, delegating, and deferring.

Systemic safety heuristics: Stabilising the improbable
Across this book, three core system techniques for managing uncertainty have emerged. They are systemic, hence not foolproof. We have to observe the effects and adapt where necessary.

A. Abstraction
General concepts like 'risk', 'incident', or 'compliance' allow systems to talk about the unknown in operational terms. These abstractions reduce anxiety and allow for distributed decision-making. But they also conceal distinctions and silence nuance.

B. Delegation
Systems delegate safety responsibilities to checklists, technologies, audits, and roles. Delegation isn't the same as transfer. The system does not become safer by outsourcing; it only appears more manageable.

C. Temporising
One of Luhmann's most underappreciated ideas is that organisations stabilise meaning by deferring decisions rather than forcing premature resolution. Procedural steps, such as reviews, sign-offs, and permits, create a time buffer that keeps systems moving while avoiding paralysis. Safety isn't managed by ever-greater precision, but by giving people the time and freedom to run safe-to-fail experiments. These temporal strategies buy space for adaptation and allow organisations to postpone risky choices until they can be addressed more meaningfully, without the illusion of perfect foresight. What emerges from these strategies is credibility rather than certainty: the confidence to act by trusting the form of the process, even when the content is incomplete.

From predictive control to procedural confidence
Luhmann teaches us to replace certainty with confidence in process. Procedures, rituals, and formalities don't guarantee safe outcomes, but they produce trustable routines. In systems that can't know everything, *credible form* is more sustainable than *guaranteed substance*. Procedure replaces truth with trust in the form. Procedures don't aim to reveal the full truth, but they define zones of acceptable blindness. Permits, audits, and training are symbolic communication acts. They stabilise expectations even when knowledge is incomplete. Formality can create social stability even under conditions of epistemic instability.

Remember:
- What we call opaqueness in systems is often a design choice;
- Control doesn't emerge from seeing more, but from framing visibility; and
- Trust in procedures is trust in limited vision.

But *form* alone is not enough. To keep learning, systems must reflect on their own framing. This is the move from structural safety to reflexive safety.

Reflexivity as safety practice
Safety professionals are observers of observation. The most powerful safety understanding often comes not from discovering new dangers, but from noticing the distinctions your system keeps making: safe/unsafe, reportable/non-reportable, deviant/normal. These distinctions are far from neutral. Each distinction carries assumptions about what matters, what is allowed to surface, and what gets suppressed. Reflexivity is about keeping those assumptions visible and open to change. So, ask yourself: *What distinctions does our system make, and what does it make invisible?*

Practical reflexivity means:
- Pausing to ask why this process is used.
- Listening for silences in reporting.
- Reframing *non-compliance* as a signal instead of a threat.
- Asking not just what happened but "Why did this count as a problem?"

This leads us toward a different kind of safety design. This one is built on flexibility, timing, and self-awareness. What follows is a toolbox for designing with uncertainty.

Designing for not-knowing

If systems are structurally blind to much of their environment, safety practice must learn to work *with* that blindness instead of against it:

- Let go of omniscience; not everything can be known;
- Build temporal slack, and design for action & pause;
- Observe the observer, and review how your system defines relevance;
- Watch the performance: What is done for safety, and what is done to appear safe?
- Every model is partial, so, keep iterating your understanding.

Safety doesn't have a stable endpoint, as it's an ongoing act of distinction and coordination. *There is no final blueprint*. Safety must remain responsive to its own evolving conditions and to the partiality of its own frames.

To see what this looks like in practice, let's turn to the next case. Northridge Public Works reveals how structural opacity can undermine learning, and how thoughtful redesign can restore system memory and meaning.

Getting out of the fog at Northridge Public Works

Northridge Public Works (NPW), one of the largest infrastructure managers in the region, oversees bridges, tunnels, locks, and pumping stations. It has more than 2,500 employees and dozens of contractors. A safety audit revealed a fundamental problem: NPW's HSE management system was no system at all. Each department defined risk differently: legal compliance, corrosion, working alone. NPW did not lack data, but it lacked shared meaning.

Contractor teams worked with performance-based contracts, focused on cost control and avoiding fines. Operational teams, on the other hand, prioritised continuity. The result was semantic friction: communication was possible, but not meaningful. As one supervisor summarised: "Contractors talk in fines. We talk in downtime. Documents describe perfection. None of that matches reality."

While manuals and tools existed, there was no integrated structure to make decisions repeatable, observable, or independent of individuals. Each team used its own language and tools, and reports from one district could not be compared to another. There was no shared memory, only loose memories.

Safety observations were made daily, but there was no second-line observation to challenge safety compliance. Dashboards tracked 'failures', but frontline workers viewed them as disconnected from reality. As one engineer put it, "What counts as a 'critical failure' depends on who you ask. It's completely arbitrary."

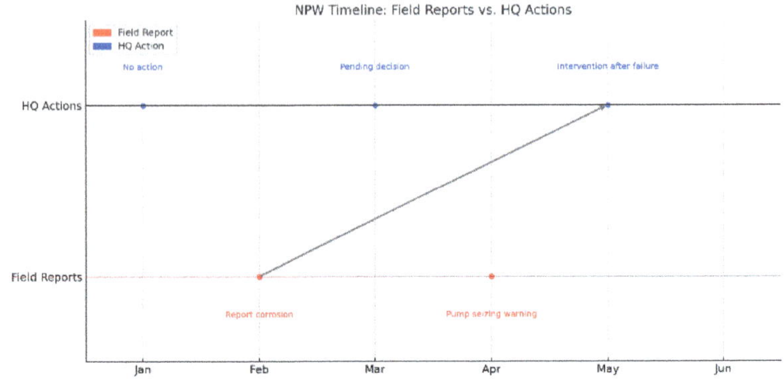

Incidents counted only as lost time. Any chance to learn from them was ignored. Head office often responded to local problems only after a disruption. Short-cycle feedback rounds were absent. Comprehension did not translate into system changes. There were no routines to convert weak signals into structural learning.

Much of NPW's practical knowledge was in the minds of long-time employees. "I know which pumps get stuck in the winter," said one engineer, "but that's not in any of the records." Remember Chapter 4: What's not part of ongoing communication doesn't exist for the organisation.

Responsibility was equally unclear. Safety consultants weren't sure who they reported to. Engineers didn't know which of the reporting apps to use to voice their concerns. Processes and documentation existed, but they didn't assign roles meaningfully in time and context. An internal memo admitted, "We lack clarity about who decides what, when, and based on what information." NPW was unable to reliably reproduce decisions. This undermined the organisation's learning and resilience.

What changed?
The external safety audit was the catalyst for reform. NPW introduced:
- A uniform HSE management system,
- Standardised risk definitions that were regularly reviewed,
- Monthly cross-functional learning reviews,
- A customer-friendly digital knowledge base,
- Clearer roles linked to mapped processes.

The goal was not Zero Harm, but self-observation: detecting blind spots, stabilising meaning and managing complexity over time. Safety, in Luhmann's terms, is not about control, but about enabling communication structures that make complexity manageable. NPW originally did not lack the will to do this, but it lacked operational completion, semantic clarity and support for long-term decisions.

From toolbox to worldview

Luhmann was never into methods, but his theory gives us a perspective on society. His theory doesn't tell us how to run a risk assessment or which KPI to track. But it can change the questions we ask and the assumptions we examine. It reframes safety from being a list of best practices to being a form of social sensemaking.

"*The aim is not to eliminate uncertainty, but to organise its effects*." – Luhmann[95]

Conclusion: Managing safety in complexity, Luhmann-style

To practice safety in a Luhmann-style is to adopt humble confidence: to trust in processes while knowing they are partial, to act decisively without pretending to know everything. Because safety professionals can't be engineers of certainty. They are practitioners of distinction, silence, and expectation, working not to control complexity, but to remain in thoughtful reaction to it. In the end, designing for not-knowing is not about surrendering to uncertainty, but about staying responsive within it. Safety is not the absence of failure, but the presence of attention.

Luhmann doesn't give us a recipe for safety, but a reorientation: a way to work within complexity rather than outside of it. But what happens when we take this idea even further: when we stop looking for the final fix, the central lever, the one true maturity model? In the last chapter, we will follow Luhmann's student Armin Nassehi's provocation that "society has no address[96]." If safety is always constructed, distributed, and in motion, then perhaps the question is not how to control it, but how to stay responsive when there is no fixed recipient for our solutions.

Chapter 14 – Managing complexity without illusion

Keywords: Functional Simplification, Paradox Management, Cartography

"*It is the tremendous dynamism of society that ensures that it ultimately remains unfazed. (...) The astonishing resilience and tolerance of error of society (happens) through the loose coupling of its components. (...) The different perspectives and logics (...) are in a permanent, mutual translation process. (...) All of this creates a highly complex conglomerate of reciprocal influences that simply cannot be traced back to causal influences.*" – Armin Nassehi[97]

After exploring how not-knowing can be designed for, and how reflexivity replaces prediction, we now reach the core tension of modern safety work. How to manage complexity without falling back on the illusion of final control? If safety is an ongoing conversation, how do we keep it meaningful in the face of overwhelming ambiguity?

The temptation of resolution

Many managers and practitioners might long to solve safety, once and for all. This impulse turns safety into a closure-seeking activity, in which hazards, controls and issues are closed and requirements are verified, leaving no room for uncertainty[98]. This closure impulse is seductive. It gives the appearance of control and accomplishment. But as Luhmann showed, what looks like resolution is often just the temporary stabilisation of complexity, until the next contradiction emerges.

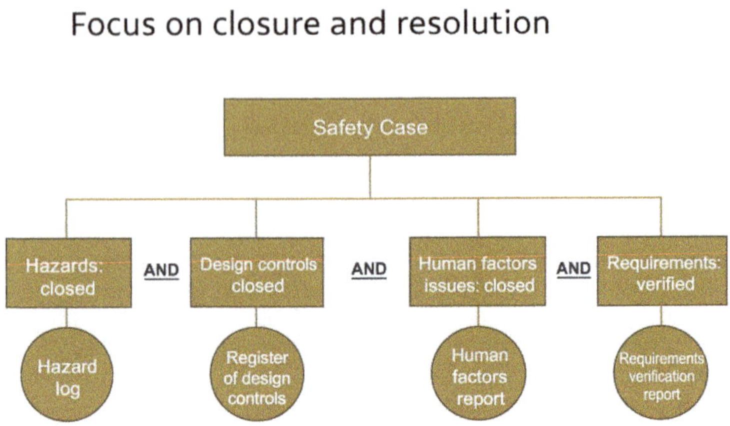

A typical approach to 'safety cases'

Safety is not a puzzle with a final solution. It reflects social complexity. We seek closure, but safety is always in motion. Not a product, but a process of adaptation to complexity.

We might ask: if we can't eliminate complexity, can we at least stay ahead of it? Luhmann's answer, refined by Armin Nassehi, is: not quite. The role of organisations is not to eliminate complexity, but to live with it, by influencing how it is perceived and distributed.

Safety as an emergent property
Luhmann teaches us that systems produce their own complexity; they don't just absorb it from the outside. His student Armin Nassehi adds[99] that organisations generate not less complexity but manage it by creating internal reductions and distinctions. Each safety solution becomes a premise for the next problem. Each decision not only resolves a moment but constructs a new blind spot. Decisions bind the future, but never fully contain it. Safety becomes a loop of decision-making that creates new risks while addressing old ones. The organisation becomes a decision machine not to simplify life, but to survive its own complexity.
Complexity also mutates through tools. We build technologies to tame it, but often these tools introduce new types of uncertainty. The burden goes from muscles to cognition, and from execution to interpretation.

Technology and its unintended consequences[100]

Uncertainty for remote control bridges

ADAM RODEWALD | USA TODAY NETWORK-Wisconsin

State transportation officials are taking steps to eventually replace some Green Bay drawbridge operators with remote control technology.

Frederick Taylor imagined organisations as rational, rule-based machines. After Taylor, we discovered that technology not only automates work, but it also transforms communication, changes the structure of organisations, and introduces new forms of vulnerability. In high-risk domains such as infrastructure, energy, and aviation, tightly coupled technical systems can be efficient, but they are also fragile. When human operators operate complex systems remotely, their decisions are limited by what the system shows them. When feedback from the system is incomplete, observational errors become fatal. The consequences are often dismissed as 'human error', while they reflect a failure of the structural coupling between technological and organisational systems.

Automation reduces the physical labour of the past; think of bridge operators who had to manually raise a bridge. But automation also increases cognitive load, fragments attention, and requires judgment in opaque situations. Computers can filter data, artificially display clarity, and support routine decisions. But they can't replace human communication, which is inherently ambiguous and intersubjective. As Luhmann reminds us[101], machines transmit information but not meaning. In complex systems, successive failures often arise not from a single failure but from the inability of systems to translate adaptively into codes such as technical, legal, and managerial. Technology must manage its own risks; organisations must regulate themselves; and society, which depends on both, can't fully manage either. The hope that we can centrally manage technological risks through organisations alone is therefore, according to Luhmann, a modern illusion.

So, what should safety professionals aim for, if control is partial and clarity is always incomplete? Perhaps the answer lies not in management as conquest, but in mapping as practice.

Safety as cartography

As we have come to the end of this book, remember that all descriptions are selections. Every map is a simplification. Safety is no exception. Every audit, checklist, and dashboard is a kind of map: it highlights some features while obscuring others. The point is not to discard these maps, but to treat them as provisional tools rather than final truths. Instead of chasing closure, we have to deal with the incompleteness of health, safety, and environment, as an ethical commitment to vigilance, adaptation, and care. The challenge is not to find the right map, but to remember that we are always mapping.

Instead of seeking singular solutions, we need formats that support plurality. Not just technical fixes, but new social architectures that can hold competing truths and codes in dialogue. For complex HSE-related problems, we can follow Nassehi's advice and install ethics commissions, interdisciplinary working groups, and other forms of multi-professional organisation that can address the problem of perspective differences. We have to learn to tolerate and endure difference together, and to incorporate each other's codes.

Managing complexity without illusion is not defeatism. If you want to call it maturity, you can: It's about working wisely with incompleteness, to remain adaptive under tension, and to never confuse the map for the terrain.

Chapter 15 – Luhmann's HSE Management

Keywords: Blind Spots, System Codes, Behaviour-Based Safety (BBS), Second-Order Observation, Symbolic Participation, Operational Closure, Gray Zones, Safety-I / Safety-II, Safety Differently, Human & Organisational Performance, Functional Differentiation, Structural Coupling, Communicative Complexity, Reflexivity

---

Gimme your data, gimme your chart
Show me the risk map, pull it apart
Gimme your logic, gimme control
Draw me a boundary, label it whole

(Chorus:)
Code for code's sake
Safety for blame's sake
Code for code's sake
Safety for blame's sake

Gimme assurance, gimme a plan
Gimme procedures, best that you can
Gimme a barrier, gimme a gate
Stamp it compliant and call it fate
(Chorus)

Gimme a culture, that hears the cues
Not just the numbers, buried in views
Keep your procedure, don't make it a cage
Safety's a story, not just a page
(Chorus)

Adapted from:
Art for Art's Sake[102] (10cc)
Graham Gouldman & Eric Stewart, 1976

Having explored the challenges of managing complexity without illusion, we now arrive at the final synthesis.
In this chapter, we ask the question: "How does Luhmann's systems theory reframe the foundations of HSE management?" Rather than giving us one more model, it changes our perspective. We move away from control as the main issue, and toward communication, complexity, and the social construction of risk and safety itself. Let's look at the case of Behavioural-Based Safety (BBS) first.

Blind spots, system codes, and the limits of behavioural safety

Perhaps this is a familiar experience for you: your organisation's leadership wants to improve safety, and safe behaviour becomes the chosen unit of analysis. A well-meaning safety manager looks for something that is empirically substantiated, rigorous, credible, and practically useful. An approach is purchased from the market, but it ultimately deviates significantly from these requirements. This tension between intention and application is structural. Luhmann would remind us that what counts as evidence, rigor, or usefulness is influenced by system-specific codes. BBS may fail from an empirical science perspective yet thrive functionally.

Despite decades of interest, the empirical basis for the widespread effectiveness of BBS is thinner than its popularity suggests. Many programmes are expressed in scientific language, but on closer inspection they are based on the rule-of-thumb doctrine of consultants rather than on replicated evidence or methodological rigor. And yet BBS is widespread. Luhmann would probably explain its success in terms of the promised reduction of complexity. BBS translates the systemic nature of workplace risks into individual psychological frameworks that feel actionable. Focus, complacency, and habit become the manageable proxies. They yield neat interventions: observe behaviour, provide feedback, retrain (repeat).

But in doing so, BBS flattens organisational complexity into the binary form of the safety checklist: safe/unsafe. It borrows words from science (observation and measurement), economics (ROI and efficiency), law (accountability), and education (training), but compresses them into a single logic for individual behavioural correction. "The problem is complacency", says the consultant, "the solution is engagement." But as Luhmann reminds us, every observation is a distinction, and every distinction creates a blind spot. The clarity BBS offers (individual error and correctable behaviour) comes at the cost of overlooking relational, structural, and temporal factors. Its promise is simplicity, but its price is oversimplification. BBS routinely treats internal states such as 'focus' or 'complacency' as visible, measurable, and causal.

By doing so, it neglects important second-order questions:

- Why is 'complacency' the chosen perspective?
- What remains unexamined when 'focus' is the central explanatory variable?
- How do our diagnostic categories constrain what can be seen, questioned, or changed?

These are reflexive questions that probe the observation itself, and they are largely absent from BBS discourse. But how does a model like BBS gain such wide uptake despite its weak empirical base? Luhmann's systems theory suggests it's not about truth, but fit. BBS functions well because it fits existing expectations across multiple subsystems, even if it fails to challenge them.

System coupling and the illusion of integration

BBS derives legitimacy from the integration of codes from different social systems:

- Behavioural models and data tracking from the science system,
- Cost savings and process efficiency from the economic system,
- Personal responsibility from the law system, and
- A structure of training and habit reinforcement from the education system.

But each of these systems operates with incompatible binaries: true/false, profitable/unprofitable, legal/illegal, informed/uninformed. Yet BBS attempts to synthesise them into a single behavioural logic, where every risk is seen as a personal mistake and every improvement as a personal change.

This creates an illusion of integration. Feedback loops, while outwardly participatory, become ritualised performances. They reproduce desired organisational narratives rather than challenging them. Participation appears widespread, but in practice is selective and depoliticised. This is what Luhmann would call symbolic stabilisation: processes that maintain structure and legitimacy without generating new ideas. What appears as learning is often reproduction. This reinforces the structures that make risk systemic rather than individual. To be fair, behavioural methods aren't inherently flawed; they're context-sensitive tools. But the more generic their application, the more symbolic their function.

When does behavioural safety really work?

Evidence from both field and large-scale studies[103] shows that BBS is effective under specific, tightly controlled conditions:

- When focused on clearly defined, observable behaviours,
- When reinforced with specific, timely feedback,
- When participation is voluntary and driven by well-trained individuals, and
- When processes are resourced and sustained over time.

These are limited design parameters. Yet many BBS implementations circumvent them by adopting generic safety campaigns, vague behavioural definitions, superficial training, or inflated observation data. More participation or more observations don't equate to better results. It's about the quality of those.

This is not an indictment of behavioural science itself. Its scientific credibility is not in question. The problem is that BBS often fails to implement the behavioural science it claims to represent. Instead, it relies on simplifications and ingrained scripts that fit neatly within existing structures but avoid confronting them. Rather than discard BBS entirely, Luhmann would invite us to observe its evolution: how it changed form to remain relevant, how it began to signal participation rather than enable change.

Reflexivity in complex systems

Luhmann's perspective helps explain the rise of BBS: it emerged at a historical moment when scientific authority, economic utility, and administrative politics were loosely coupled. But even that loose coupling proved fragile. Over time, BBS drifted away from its scientific roots. It adapted to market demands through oversimplification and lost internal mechanisms for critical reflection and learning. What emerged was a pattern of functional decay. Participation became symbolic, and as feedback became routine, systemic complexity was filtered out.

To revitalise or move beyond BBS, we need to reconnect behavioural safety with theory, empirical evidence, and second order thinking. We also need to equip leaders not just to motivate but to transform systems. Governance needs to be rebuilt so that safety efforts are supported by processes rather than 'personality'. Finally, we need to support reflexivity, where tools, models, and metrics are open to questioning and revision. Reflexivity is a survival mechanism in complex systems. Without it, safety programmes harden into rituals that no longer correspond to lived complexity.

In complex systems, simplification is tempting, but also dangerous. Safety can't be reduced to awareness, attention, or complacency. It's a dynamic outcome of interdependent behaviours, tools, structures, and cultures. To manage it well, we need to become as alert to our blind spots as we are to our checklists.

As we close the circle, the question becomes: what kind of safety work is possible when we stop pretending complexity can be controlled? Here, Luhmann offers a way to see how systems construct, manage, and obscure their own risks.

What does Luhmann's Systems Theory bring to HSE management?

Luhmann's systems theory helps HSE professionals look beyond procedures and compliance checklists. Luhmann encourages us to examine how organisations stabilise expectations and how safety is continually negotiated, instead of simply imposed from above. Safety goes beyond the rulebook. It's a dynamic process of managing expectations, behaviour, and uncertainty within formal and informal structures. A few *Luhmannian* lessons for HSE management:

- Organisations are not closed feedback loops from command and control to execution and back again. HSE management systems exist in relation to the environment: reactions to accidents, stakeholder pressure, and regulatory standards. HSE professionals maintain the internal order of rules, procedures, and audits while also adapting to these external dynamics. Although HSE systems often rely on formal expectations such as PPE policies and Stop Work procedures, these procedures can't cover every scenario. Deviations from them are, therefore, not simply mistakes. Workarounds, shortcuts or silent non-compliance can point to practical needs or design gaps. Effective HSE management requires observing both formal compliance and informal adaptations: "how things are really done". Therefore, we have to keep track of how procedures are actually implemented on the work floor, not just whether forms are filled out. Systems run on interpretation. The gap between *form and function* is a space to be understood.

- In Luhmann's theory, individuals (employees, managers) interact with the system's operations through communication. Systems observe and adapt through how they communicate. Workers and engineers are constantly interpreting, adapting and translating procedures into action. The question "Why did the employee not follow the rule?" is the wrong question. Better to ask: "How did they understand the situation and why did this rule not fit?"

- Remember: although rules, procedures and audits are very often necessary for HSE management, especially for high-risk, too much formalisation undermines adaptability. No checklist can handle every critical moment.

HSE management is characterised by tensions between:

Stability (formal)	and	Flexibility (informal)
Standard procedure	and	Workarounds
Job descriptions	and	Role adaptation
Safety audits	and	Peer learning, storytelling
Incident reports	and	Informal debriefings

- In HSE management, we often equate responsibility with blame, especially for non-compliance. Luhmann points out that responsibility is about absorbing uncertainty: interpreting ambiguous situations and making them manageable. Frontline workers often bear the real burden of this uncertainty absorption (e.g. grabbing the phone and calling a colleague during abnormal conditions), even if they are not formally responsible. HSE systems should support those who absorb uncertainty, not just punish them when results are disappointing. This means: build trust and discretion into HSE roles, not just compliance pressure.

- Organisations must project safety to external observers like regulators, media, and customers, even when internal practices are less tidy. This creates a performance layer where internal mess is hidden behind clean paperwork. But exaggerating the appearance of safety can backfire. If internal realities such as near misses, stress, or risk taking are suppressed to protect the image, learning stops. Therefore, encourage truth-finding over image management. This calls for a supervisory system that's structured for understanding instead of box-ticking compliance.

- Safety professionals are boundary managers. They translate external expectations (laws, audits, and branch safety alerts) into internal practices. They explain internal constraints (production pressures and limited resources) to external actors. These roles are inherently conflicting and require judgment, discretion, and informal relationships. Rules alone are not enough. Support must include soft skills, networking, and autonomy.

- Sometimes, breaking a rule is what keeps people safest. For example, bypassing automation to prevent an accident. Luhmann called this the grey zone: actions that are technically illegal but functionally necessary. We have to recognise that breaking rules is not always bad; sometimes it's a temporary solution that keeps people safe. We have to follow up on these exceptions and learn from them instead of simply punishing them. So, create safe channels to discuss deviations without fear of reprisal.

- In HSE, communication is not just about sending reminders or updating standard procedures. We must establish shared expectations, enable horizontal knowledge sharing (e.g. peer-to- peer safety tips), and recognise weak signals before they lead to failures. Strict vertical reporting lines can't quickly handle surprises. Systems need to facilitate informal conversations, toolbox discussions, story sharing and consultation, and value soft signals as much as lagging indicators.

- HSE leadership is not about just giving orders and enforcing rules. Rather, we must translate operational pressures into safety ideals, mediate conflicting priorities, and build trust. Leaders need to balance expectations from above and below them, balance enforcement with empathy, maintain credibility through honesty and support rather than through command.

- HSE management systems are never fully coherent. Tensions are inevitable: safety versus productivity, compliance versus innovation, roles versus situations. Formal rules can't resolve every conflict. Informal mechanisms like alliances, discretion, and backchannels are needed to keep things moving. Rather than seeing these as corruption or failure, we should treat them as adaptive responses to real complexity. The goal is adaptively working safely. Luhmann reminds us that organisations don't survive by enforcing perfect order, but by managing contradictions and adapting flexibly. In HSE, this means designing systems that can evolve instead of just comply. It also means accepting that informal behaviour is inevitable and managing it safely and recognising working safely as a dynamic property instead of a static state.

- When building or improving an HSE system, Luhmann encourages us to look beyond the checklist and ask: "How do people actually support 'working safely' here: formally, informally, and everything in between?" That's where resilience begins.

A Luhmannian Perspective on the New View of Safety

The contrast between 'safety paradigms' is a study in distinctions. Luhmann would ask: "What system dynamics do these views stabilise? And what do they exclude?"

Within safety science and practice, there remains an ongoing debate between the self-proclaimed 'New View of Safety' and more traditional approaches to safety management. Erik Hollnagel, author of Safety-I and Safety-II, already stated in his 2014 book that both approaches are valuable[104]. However, the debate often stagnates because both sides operate from different observational codes.

Safety-I focuses on preventing things from going wrong. The emphasis is on errors, deviations, and measurable shortcomings (incidents, injuries).
Safety-II focuses on how things go *well*. It investigates how people and systems succeed under pressure and how everyday performance adapts to complexity.

Luhmann argued that observation always involves a distinction between what is selected as meaningful and what is excluded. When we define safety, we observe through specific systems with their own binary codes, such as:

- Safe vs. unsafe,
- Cooperative vs. non-cooperative, and
- Normal vs. abnormal

Crucially, Luhmann reminds us that there is no privileged vantage point from which to observe 'safety'. Each 'paradigm' constructs its own version of what matters. The debate between Safety-I and Safety-II is often framed as a factual dispute between what works and what doesn't. But from a systems-theoretical perspective, these are functionally different observations. Rather than choosing between them, systems theory encourages us to ask: What function does each paradigm serve within the broader system?

Safety-II is often criticised for being vague or difficult to measure. But this critique shows a change in the guiding code of the safety system itself. Instead of asking, "Was there harm?", Safety-II asks, "How did we succeed despite pressure, complexity, or surprise?" In Luhmann's terms, it transforms both the medium and the form of safety communication.

For example:
- Safety-I is based on reportable events and KPIs.
- Safety-II produces stories, reflections, and practices that may not fit into traditional categories but still influence how work is done.

Each paradigm has its blind spots. What one sees clearly, the other may entirely overlook.
Luhmann shifts the question from "Which 'paradigm' is true?" to "What distinctions are useful for the continuation of the system?" The value of a theory lies in its capacity to generate new observations:
- Safety-I enables accountability, standardisation, and the creation of visible artefacts.
- Safety-II enables learning, adaptability, and system reflexivity.

From this perspective, both paradigms provide partial answers—an expected feature of how systems manage complexity.

What does this mean for the safety professional?
- Use Safety-I to stabilise systems, track performance, and meet regulatory standards.
- Use Safety-II to understand how work actually happens, and to investigate adaptation and weak signals.

Don't expect either to be complete, but use them as complementary tools. When in doubt, ask: What distinctions am I making? What am I excluding?

Comparing contemporary safety approaches with Luhmann
In recent decades, several approaches have challenged existing safety management approaches that focus on error reduction, compliance, and prevention of negative consequences. Among the most influential are Erik Hollnagel's Safety-I and Safety-II[105], Sidney Dekker's Safety Differently[106], and the Human and Organisational Performance (HOP) movement associated with Todd Conklin[107], Bob Edwards, and Andrea Baker[108]. These so-called "New View" perspectives look at how work actually happens, how people adapt under pressure, and how to learn from both success and failure. The table below compares these approaches in several areas: focus, understanding of human roles, view of risk, management implications, and learning orientation.

While each has its own strengths, they share a change from blame and error to understanding systems, variability, and human adaptability.

	Safety-I &-II	**Safety Differently**	**HOP**
Main idea	Focus on preventing what goes wrong (SI). Focus on enabling what goes right (SII).	Safety is not the absence of accidents, but the presence of capacities.	Focus on understanding how people adapt and perform work safely in complex systems.
Focus	From reactive (Safety-I) to proactive (Safety-II); from error to resilience.	From control & compliance to enabling autonomy & local sensemaking.	Understanding normal work variation and local rationality.
Role of humans	From liability (error source) to asset (source of resilience).	Humans are the adaptable part of the system, not the problem to be controlled.	Humans manage variability and bridge systemic gaps.
View on risk	Risk emerges from complexity & is managed by strengthening system performance.	Risk is relational and constructed through oversimplified narratives.	Risk stems from misunderstanding system functioning and operator intent.
Management implication	Support flexible performance, build resilience, monitor everyday work.	De-emphasise compliance, re-emphasise dialogue and reflection.	Promote learning environments, reduce blame, support learning from normal work.
Learning focus	Learn from what goes right to understand capacity for success.	Learn from front-line expertise and knowledge.	Learn from normal operations and adaptations.

Table: Contemporary safety approached compared

How Luhmann's HSE Management differs

Niklas Luhmann's theory, on the other hand, doesn't contain a new method for HSE management, but rather a way to observe how organisations construct, communicate, and reproduce the meaning of health, safety, and environment. Luhmann's approach is not normative or interventionist, but it looks at systemic achievements and at the way in which organisations reduce the complexity of the environment and stabilise expectations through recursive communication.

Where the New View focuses on adaptation at the front line, Luhmann focuses on organisational sensemaking instead: how systems define what counts as 'safe', what counts as a 'deviation', and how decisions are shaped by internal codes (e.g., legal/illegal, safe/unsafe, reportable/non-reportable). Luhmann points to the operational closure of systems. They don't control each other directly. They can only irritate or influence each other through *structurally linked communication*.

Safety, in this view, is an emergent property of communicative processes under complex conditions.
Luhmann's HSE management is therefore not a replacement for practical tools from e.g. HOP or Safety Differently, but a *reflective view*. It helps us to understand why certain forms of HSE management become dominant, which risks are made visible or invisible, and how organisational structures promote or hinder learning, adaptation and trust. While the New View functions within systems to improve them, Luhmann observes systems from the outside to understand how safety becomes possible or impossible in the first place.

Final Thought
Instead of a new toolbox, Luhmann gives us a mirror in which we see safety as a communicative achievement, fragile and ongoing. The task of the HSE professional is to keep complexity visible, and liveable.

Acknowledgements

Writing may seem like a solo activity, but this book is anything but a solo effort. What contributed to it were many conversations, collaborations, support, and encouragement from people across different walks of life, at home, at work, and beyond.

First, thank you to Leonie, Tim, and Fianne. Your love, patience, and presence kept me grounded throughout this project, especially during the moments when I was buried in theory or staring at a blank page. You've supported me far more than any safety model or footnote ever could.

To my parents, thank you for taking me to our family in Germany so often, so I could practice my German. Also, thanks for encouraging me to pursue education and to stay curious. My father, who's no longer with us, taught me the value of doing something you truly enjoy. That example stayed with me.

To my colleagues: thank you for asking the right questions, challenging assumptions, and reminding me that safety is lived instead of just discussed. I also want to thank my employer, Rijkswaterstaat, for making space for the research that helped start this book, particularly through the opportunity to study at Delft University of Technology.

A thank-you goes to Ronald van Eerdenburgh, a long-time independently contracted safety professional, who persistently told me I had to write this book. Ronald, you were right. *Dankjewel!*

At Delft University of Technology, I've been lucky to be part of an academic environment that welcomed cross-disciplinary thinking. It gave me the tools, and the necessary friction, to make sense of complex ideas in practical ways. Thank you, Frank Guldenmund, for your guidance during and beyond my time at the Graduate School.

Thanks also to Carsten Busch, for being the kind of critical reader who sharpens your thinking instead of shutting it down. Your suggestions, both in theory and LP records, have made a real difference. I hereby grant you the honorary title: *Professor Prog*. Oh, and thanks for your help with solving the layout in the final stage! Any remaining errors are mine and mine alone.

To Jos Villevoye, thanks for your writing, and calling safety a dysfunctional concept, which made me think! And thank you for taking the photo that I could use on the back cover.

Thanks to Robert Jan de Boer, for connecting me to a broader safety community through Safety Speakers. I hope your Master of Modern Safety Management programme becomes everything it deserves to be, and more.

I would like to thank Jean-Christophe Le Coze for his inspiring work on a constructivist and broad approach to safety, as well as for the valuable collaboration on our joint research project.

Also, a thank-you to Mr. Sociological Safety, Rob Jones, who was kind enough to make a Venn-like Living Map for chapter 7.

Finally, a sincere thank you to Professor Stefan Kühl. Your writing helped bring Luhmann's complex theory into the real world of organisations. Without your work, this project wouldn't have taken the shape it did.

This book is the result of an enormous amount of interactions. To everyone who contributed in big or small ways and is not yet mentioned above: thank you.

Suggested reading

If you, after reading my book, want to find out more about Luhmann's work, here's my list:

For beginners
Here's an easy and fun way to start; a book with cartoons about Luhmann's philosophy (in German):

Müller, J., Lorenz, A. (2016), *Niklas Luhmann: Philosophie für Einsteiger*, Paderborn: Brill | Fink.

For a somewhat friendly description of the theory
A good introduction to Luhmann's theory for people who, like me, are intimidated at first by the sheer density of his writing:

Kneer, G., Nassehi, A. (2001), *Niklas Luhmanns Theorie sozialer Systeme: Eine Einführung*, Stuttgart: UTB.(German)

In my opinion, the friendliest of Luhmann's own introductions is this collection of lectures:

Luhmann, N. (2013), *Introduction to Systems Theory*, Cambridge/Malden: Polity Press.

For applications
An application of Luhmann's theory to organisations (in German):

Muster, J., Hermwille, A., Kapitzky, J. (2024), *Lehren von Luhmann: Angewandte Systemtheorie: Pragmatische Lösungsansätze für Organisationen*, Verl: managerSeminare.

Stefan Kühl has many books that build on Luhmann's work. They are available in both German and English. These are my favourites:

Kühl, S. (2018), Influencing Organisational Culture - A Very Brief Introduction, Princeton: Organisational Dialogue Press.

Kühl, S. (2021), Organisations – A Short Introduction, Princeton: Organisational Dialogue Press.

Kühl, S. (2022), Useful Illegality: The Benefits of Breaking the Rules in Organisations, Princeton: Organisational Dialogue Press.

Some of them (now thirteen, and counting) even can be read for free online:
https://organisationaldialoguepress.com/books2/

Notes

[1] Illustration of Luhmann's System/Umwelt distinction. Origin unknown; it was on a Luhmann-themed T-shirt that appears to no longer be available.
[2] Esser, H.M. (2017), Der Unsterbliche - Zum 90. von Niklas Luhmann, *The European – Das Debatten-Magazin*, https://www.theeuropean.de/politik/der-unsterbliche
[3] www.untersoziologen.com
[4] Photo of Niklas Luhmann copyright Professor Dr. Detlef Horster, used with permission. Source: https://www.ndr.de/geschichte/koepfe/Soziologische-Systemtheorie-von-Niklas-Luhmann-ein-Ueberblick,luhmann132.html
[5] Hagen, W. (ed., 2004), *Warum haben Sie keinen Fernseher, Herr Luhmann? Letzte Gespräche mit Niklas Luhmann*, Berlin: Kulturverlag Kadmos.
[6] Luhmann, N. (2004), *Einführung in die Systemtheorie*, 2nd edition, Heidelberg: Carl-Auer.
[7] Especially Parsons' framework as explained in e.g. Parsons, T. (1961), *The Social System*, London: The Free Press of Glencoe.
[8] Deming, W.E. (2018), *The New Economics for Industry, Government, Education*, third edition, Cambridge/London: The MIT Press.
[9] Ibidem, page 65.
[10] Thirty-five years later, this line by Monty Python was used for a paper:
Cook, R.I, Nemeth, C.P. (2010), "Those found responsible have been sacked": some observations on the usefulness of error, in: *Cogn Tech Work*, Vol. 12: pp. 87–93.
[11] Monty Python and the Holy Grail opening credits, copied from https://members.tripod.com/dracenfire_/grailcredits.htm
[12] Luhmann, N. (1991), *Soziologie des Risikos*, Berlin/New York: Walter de Gruyter. The quote is on page 210.
[13] Luhmann, N. (2003), *Soziologie des Risikos*, chapter 10, section II, Berlin/New York: Walter de Gruyter.
[14] Luhmann, N. (1991), *Soziologie des Risikos*, Berlin/New York: Walter de Gruyter. The quote is on page 208.
[15] Luhmann, N. (1991), *Soziologie des Risikos*, Berlin/New York: Walter de Gruyter. The quote and the text that inspires this paragraph is on pages 210 and 211.
[16] This picture of an oil refinery in Canada is an illustration that has nothing to do with the described case. Picture source: https://upload.wikimedia.org/wikipedia/commons/0/01/Oil_refinery_canada.jpg; licensed under the Creative Commons Attribution-Share Alike 2.0 Generic license.

[17] Hollnagel, E. (2014), *Safety-I and Safety-II - The Past and Future of Safety Management*, London: CRC Press.
[18] Luhmann, N. (1981), *Soziologische Aufklärung 3 - Soziales System, Gesellschaft, Organisation*, Opladen: Westdeutscher Verlag.
[19] Woods, D.D. (2017), *STELLA - Report from the SNAFUcatchers Workshop on Coping With Complexity*, Brooklyn NY, March 14-16, 2017, https://bpb-us-w2.wpmucdn.com/u.osu.edu/dist/4/103481/files/2021/04/stellareportfinalfinal.pdf
[20] Epstude, K., Roese, N.J. (2008), The Functional Theory of Counterfactual Thinking, In: *Pers Soc Psychol Rev.,* Vol. 12, Issue 2: 168–192.
[21] Bergström, J. (2017), Three analytical traps in incident investigation, YouTube-video, Lund: Lund University Human Factors and Systems Safety. https://www.youtube.com/watch?v=TqaFT-0cY7U
[22] Hollnagel, E., Woods, D.D, Leveson, N. (Eds.) (2006), *Resilience Engineering – Concepts and Precepts*; Boca Raton, Florida: CRC Press.
[23] Picture: *Safe or Unsafe Behavior Game* at TinyTap.com. I found the examples through googling the phrase "Is it safe?".
[24] Picture by Niels Kim, WikiMedia Commons, Creative Commons Attribution-Share Alike 3.0 Unported license. https://commons.wikimedia.org/wiki/File:Zaandenuylbrug.jpg
[25] Hollnagel, E. (2012), *FRAM: The Functional Resonance Analysis Method - Modelling Complex Socio-technical Systems*, Boca Raton: CRC Press.
[26] Leveson, N.G. (2012), *Engineering a Safer World: Systems Thinking Applied to Safety*, Cambridge: The MIT Press.
[27] If you work in HSE or risk management, you may have come across Dave Snowden's Cynefin® framework. It distinguishes between obvious, complicated, complex, chaotic, or disordered contexts. It gives pragmatic guidance for acting under uncertainty. Snowden's more recent work expands this into a broader naturalistic theory of sense-making. His approach surfaces the conditions under which people perceive what is possible, necessary, or legitimate. Through mapping actors, constraints, and evolving narratives, it enables action in *liminal zones* where failure is possible, but learning is still safe. Safety, in this view, is a fluid *affordance landscape* formed by entangled assemblages of people, tools, and meaning.
My own approach in this book is informed by a different tradition: Niklas Luhmann's sociological systems theory. Where Snowden focuses on how people make sense of complexity and act within it, Luhmann examines how social systems construct

meaning, including how distinctions like safe/unsafe, or responsible/irresponsible, become stabilised over time. Luhmann didn't aim to manage complexity, but to reveal how simplification itself enables communication and coordination, while inevitably producing exclusions and blind spots.
These two perspectives arise from different ontologies (grounded in naturalistic sense-making and embodied action, versus in second-order observation and systems theory) but they are not incompatible. Together, they help us understand both how people act in complexity and how those actions are framed, interpreted, and legitimated across systems that speak different codes, such as law, politics, media, and economics.
For Snowden's most recent work on complexity and futures, see:
Snowden, D. (2024), *As through a glass darkly: a complex systems approach to futures*, in: R. Poli (Ed.), *Handbook of Futures Studies* (pp. 48–63), Edward Elgar.
Open access:
https://www.elgaronline.com/downloadpdf/edcollchap-oa/book/9781035301607/book-part-9781035301607-11.pdf
License: Creative Commons BY-NC-ND 4.0.

[28] Luhmann, N. (2013), *Introduction to Systems Theory*, Cambridge/Malden: Polity Press.

[29] Luhmann, N. (2004), Einführung in die Systemtheorie, Heidelberg: Carl-Auer-Systeme Verlag. The passage that inspires this paragraph is on page 174.

[30] Luhmann, N. (1983), *Legitimation durch Verfahren*, Frankfurt am Main: Suhrkamp Verlag. Pages 225 and 226.

[31] Ibidem, page 226.

[32] Luhmann, N. (2001), *Aufsätze und Reden,* Stuttgart: Reclam. The quote is on page 111.

[33] Onderzoeksraad voor Veiligheid (2023), *Dodelijk ongeval in ladingtank van chemicaliëntanker - Lessen uit het voorval aan boord van de NCC SAFA*, Den Haag: OvV.

[34] A design that can help prevent inadequate process models to cause unsafe control actions is given by:
Leveson, N.G., Thomas, J.P. (2018), *STPA Handbook*, Cambridge MA: The MIT Press. Specifically, page 45.
https://psas.scripts.mit.edu/home/get_file.php?name=STPA_Handbook.pdf

[35] Luhmann, N. (2003), *Soziologie des Risikos*, chapter 1, section IV, Berlin/New York: Walter de Gruyter.

[36] Luhmann, N. (2003), *Soziologie des Risikos*, page 39, Berlin/New York: Walter de Gruyter.

[37] Barry Turner called this the 'decoy problem'.
Turner, B. (1978), *Man-made disasters*, Wykeham Publications.

[38] Brinkmann, U. (2011), *Die unsichtbare Faust des Marktes - Betriebliche Kontrolle und Koordination im Finanzmarktkapitalismus*, Berlin: edition sigma.
[39] Photo by GS GmbH.
[40] Luhmann, N. (2003), *Soziologie des Risikos*, Berlin/New York: Walter de Gruyter. The Lapland example is on page 40.
[41] Luhmann, N. (1991), *Soziologie des Risikos*, Berlin/New York: Walter de Gruyter. I paraphrase Luhmann here. The original quote translates into English like this: "*The primary risk of the decision at issue is offset, supplemented, and mitigated by a second risk, but since the second risk is also a risk, it may also be increased. The additional and mitigating risk may be that prevention may be entirely unnecessary: You chase yourself through the forest day after day to stay healthy and ultimately crash your plane. Or the prevention proves to be causally ineffective. Or it was merely a useful fiction of encouragement. The risk-avoidance risk still remains a risk.*"
[42] Luhmann, N. (2003), *Soziologie des Risikos*, chapter 10, section I, Berlin/New York: Walter de Gruyter.
[43] Luhmann, N. (1991), *Soziologie des Risikos*, Berlin/New York: Walter de Gruyter. The quote is on page 216.
[44] It's originally a WikiMedia Commons picture, now found here: https://itoldya420.getarchive.net/media/deepwater-horizon-offshore-drilling-unit-on-fire-2010-cropped-3-to-2-e7cf87
[45] Rae, A.J., Mcdermid, J.A., Alexander, R.D., Nicholson, M. (2014), Probative blindness: how safety activity can fail to update beliefs about safety, in: *9th IET International Conference on System Safety and Cyber Security*. As well as: Rae, A.J., Alexander, R.D. (2017), Probative Blindness and False Assurance about Safety, in: *Safety Science* Vol. 92, February 2017, pp. 190-204.
[46] Luhmann, N. (2018), *Systemtheorie der Gesellschaft*, Berlin: Suhrkamp Verlag. Luhmann writes about communication on pages 146 and further.
[47] Luhmann, N. (2021), *Die Grenzen der Verwaltung*, Berlin: Suhrkamp Verlag. The quote is on page 58.
[48] See endnote 45.
[49] Luhmann, N. (1983), *Legitimation durch Verfahren*, Frankfurt am Main: Suhrkamp Verlag. On page 2 he writes: "*Factual, currently conscious consensus on relevant decision-making content is empirically undeterminable, and indeed completely unthinkable in highly complex societies with rapidly fluctuating regulations. One must then resort to mystifications such as "collective background consciousness" or imagine a consensus-building potential that can never be updated. A solution to these problems must be found—if not within the framework of*

the conventional understanding of legitimacy, then with the help of another. My suggestion is to temporalize the concept of legitimacy with the help of learning theory and regain the content-dependent certainty that it provides through the differentiation and reconnection of a majority of procedures. This is precisely where I see the political achievement of the bourgeois revolution. My aim was to demonstrate this achievement in all its formality, temporal structure, and institutional complexity—in an era that is once again becoming naive in political matters and beginning to replace structural achievements with good intentions."

[50] Photo of woman in PPE by pixabay.com, Creative Commons CC0 1.0 Universal Public Domain Dedication license.

[51] Dekker, S. (2017), *The Safety Anarchist*, Abingdon/New York: Routledge.

[52] Hopkins, A. (2019), *Organising for safety – How structure creates culture*, Sydney: CCH Australia Limited.

[53] Neelis, M. (2023), Van markt tenzij naar de markt en wij, keynote, *Contractmanagementdag 2023*, Zeist: NEVI.

[54] Kühl, S., Bisky, J. (2025), Wenn die Bürokratie stört - Ein Gespräch mit Stefan Kühl über Ministerien, Entbürokratisierung und die Fallen der Bürokratiekritik, in: *Soziopolis*, https://www.soziopolis.de/wenn-die-buerokratie-stoert.html

[55] For specific examples: Dekker, S. (2002), *Compliance Capitalism – How Free Markets Have Led to Unfree, Overregulated Workers*, Abingdon/New York: Routledge.

[56] Luhmann, N. (1994), *Die Wirtschaft der Gesellschaft*, p. 114, Frankfurt am Main: Suhrkamp Verlag. On pages 54-55, he writes: "*An understanding of the economy that begins with payments as the basic operations of the system can treat everything that otherwise functions as a fundamental concept of economic theory—such as production, exchange, distribution, capital, and labor—as a derivative. Above all, this approach makes the difference between value and price understandable as a moment of the differentiation of the system. Within the system, values represent the social relevance of economic activity, while prices represent the system's internal autopoiesis. For as soon as payments must be made, prices are necessary that enable expectations regarding the amount to be paid to be formed and communicated about. The autopoiesis of the system thus becomes independent of an agreement on the "real value" of goods and services; and above all, it becomes independent of obligations of gratitude (and thus also of the fear of the emergence of obligations of gratitude) that could arise from one side providing more value (or, in its opinion, more value) than the other. Every effectively made payment*

---

has a price-forming effect and thus acquires a secondary effect at the level of structure formation; In addition to regenerating payment options in the hands of the recipient, it also enables the formation of expectations about which payments are considered for which goods and services. The regeneration of payments through payments automatically creates structures that, in turn, become conscious as contingent and variable, thus being susceptible to influence through interaction (bargaining) and organisation, because the autopoiesis of the economy is secured on a monetary basis."

[57] Le Coze, J.C. (2019), How safety culture can make us think, in: *Safety Science*, Vol. 118, October 2019, Pages 221-229.

[58] Luhmann, N. (1984), *Soziale Systeme - Grundriß einer allgemeinen Theorie*, Frankfurt am Main: Suhrkamp Verlag. I paraphrase Luhmann here. The original quote translates as: "*With (...) any meaning, an incomprehensibly high level of complexity (...) is made available for the operations of psychological or social systems. Meaning, on the one hand, ensures that these operations cannot destroy complexity, but rather continuously generate it through the use of meaning. (...) The form of meaning compels selection, a choice from a range of possibilities, but each selection in turn contains a reference to more or less probable possible connections."*

[59] Kühl, S. (2011), *Organisationen – Eine sehr kurze Einführung*, Wiesbaden: Springer/VS Verlag. On pages 136-157, Stefan Kühl describes the organisational theatre as a façade; a carefully constructed and managed representation of how an organisation wants to be perceived. Drawing on neo-institutionalist theory, he writes that façades serve to secure legitimacy by projecting coherence, competence, and coupling with societal values, even when internal operations are contradictory or chaotic. The façade performs protective, representational, and symbolic functions. Organisations manage these façades through press offices, corporate design, and selective transparency, often engaging in what Kühl, following Nils Brunsson, calls 'necessary hypocrisy' or 'double talk', where external communication is decoupled from internal practice. The theater metaphor was originally developed by Erving Goffman:
Goffman, E. (1956), *The Presentation of Self in Everyday Life*, University of Edinburgh Press.
Coincidentally, Sidney Dekker's new book with the title *Safety Theater* came out during the writing of my book.

[60] Volandis (2025), Pubquiz over veiligheid nu ook voor kleine bedrijven, in: *Bouwtotaal*.

https://www.bouwtotaal.nl/2025/06/pubquiz-over-veiligheid-nu-ook-voor-kleine-bedrijven/

[61] See the books of Scott Geller, for instance:
Geller, E.S., Veazie, B. (2017), *The Motivation to Actively Care - How You Can Make it Happen*, New York: Morgan James Publishing.

[62] Luhmann, N. (2011), *Organisation und Entscheidung*, Third Edition, pp. 39-80, Wiesbaden: Springer/VS. Luhmann reconceptualised organisations as autopoietic systems; self-reproducing structures constituted through the recursive communication of decisions rather than by goals, structures, or individuals. He critiqued traditional organisational theories for relying on essentialist or input/output models that can't resolve the paradoxes of identity and difference inherent in social systems. Instead of looking at *what* an organisation is, Luhmann studies *how* it reproduces itself through operational closure and internal distinctions. Organisations, like all social systems, are operationally closed: they only process information they themselves generate through communicative events. Their boundaries are defined by their own decision-making operations, which simultaneously reduce and regenerate uncertainty. Each decision references prior ones and anticipates future ones, producing a *recursive network* that enables systemic learning rather than direct environmental adaptation. Power, membership, and structure within organisations are all second-order effects of this process. This approach replaces the notion of organisation as a fixed entity with one of ongoing, contingent differentiation maintained through internally meaningful communication. Thus, organisations are not simply influenced by their environment but they construct their environments through the distinctions their communication makes possible.

[63] Luhmann, N. (2016), *Der neue Chef*, Frankfurt am Main: Suhrkamp Verlag. An example of the importance of this statement is on page 65-66: "*A lack of information is often the fate of the superior who is, at best, a half-colleague. Their loyalty and discretion are difficult to secure through purely collegial means, and their wider communications are difficult to control, and therefore, cautious restraint is appropriate in dealings with them – especially when they use the unfamiliar form of address "Mr. Colleague," to demonstrate inequality through the way they emphasize equality. However, more skilled superiors are quite capable of playing the roles of superior and colleague side by side, albeit not simultaneously, in changing situations. They have their accessible hours when*

their role as superiors goes through a latent phase, so to speak, and a frank discussion, as among colleagues, is possible."

[64] Luhmann, N. (1968), *Vertrauen - Ein Mechanismus der Reduktion sozialer Komplexität*, Stuttgart: F. Enke Verlag. In Chapter 4, Luhmann describes that trust is a social mechanism for managing uncertainty. Trust enables individuals to commit to actions based on the expectation that others will behave reliably, despite the inherent unpredictability of social life. When such expectations fail, regret often follows; this reveals the risk embedded in trusting. Still, without trust, much of social coordination would be irrational or impossible. Trust simplifies decision-making by reducing the complexity of the world: it allows people to act without analysing every contingency, instead relying on generalised expectations shaped by culture, routine, or experience. Importantly, trust often operates automatically or habitually, especially in roles where decisions must be made under uncertainty, such as management, where trust functions like an advance credit which enables action in the absence of full information. While people may rationalise their trust after the fact to preserve self-image, the act itself remains a calculated risk that extends beyond available evidence. Because the real world is too complex to fully anticipate or control, trust is frequently managed by cues like tone or subtle behaviour which signals reliability or its breach. Trust depends on thresholds: when violated, even slightly, it can collapse. This fragility reflects trust's function as a simplification of reality. Trust substitutes external uncertainty with internal confidence, allowing social systems and individuals to tolerate ambiguity. Yet for Luhmann, this didn't make trust a final solution; it remained part of the problem of complexity itself: a necessary strategy for dealing with the risks of living in an unpredictable world.

[65] The Trust Map is a Venn-like diagram based on the conceptual framework articulated by Rob Jones. It draws from field theory and semantic structuring grounded in the work of social psychologist Kurt Lewin (1890-1947). The triadic structure reflects Kurt Lewin's notion of a 'life space', where perception and behavior are influenced by the dynamic interaction between the individual and their environment. The diagram's shape is an 'inside-out' transformation of the traditional 3x3 grid, which, while useful for classification, falls short of capturing the recursive, relational, and fractal nature of lived meaning.

This approach aligns with Lewin's emphasis on contextual dynamism and interdependence within psychological life spaces. The core of the diagram, where all three perspectives converge, stands as a representation of holistic meaning-making; interpretation is the result of the recursive interaction between perception, position, and principle. For more information, visit Jones' blog (https://inclusiveworks.medium.com/the-semantic-optics-of-reality-5f1e11fa9858) or connect with him on LinkedIn, through Venningmachine.com.

[66] The news item about the Eternit case was featured in Dutch news: *NOS Journaal*, June 17th 2025. The photo is a screenshot I took when watching the newsitem.

[67] See also recent research on 'local ingenuity', e.g. Leonie Boskeljon-Horst's PhD dissertation:
Boskeljon-Horst, L. (2023), *The Bogeyman Unveiled - Safety and effectiveness within the Royal Netherlands Air Force*, [Dissertation (TU Delft), Delft University of Technology].
https://doi.org/10.4233/uuid:315bdb50a76b-4ce6-aa2b-fab05aa679b3

[68] Luhmann, N. (1976), *Funktionen und Folgen formaler Organisation*, 3rd edition, Berlin: Duncker & Humblot, p. 304-314.

[69] Kleist, H. von (2020 [1910]), *Prinz von Homburg*, Frankfurt am Main: outlook Verlag.
I was triggered to read von Kleist's play when reading descriptions of the *Prinz von Homburg Dilemma* in a book by sociologist Horst Bosetzky:
Bosetzky, H. (2018), *Mikropolitik – Netzwerke und Karrieren*, Wiesbaden: SpringerVS .

[70] Portrait of Prince Friedrich of Homburg by Pieter Nason's studio, WikiMedia Commons.
https://en.wikipedia.org/wiki/File:Friedrich_II_van_Hessen-Homburg_(1633-1708),_by_studio_of_Pieter_Nason.jpg

[71] Luhmann, N. (1976), *Funktionen und Folgen formaler Organisation*, 3rd edition, Berlin: Duncker & Humblot. The section on page 256 translates into English as: *"In order to reconcile these minor sanctions with the membership rule, the violation must be interpreted in a specific way. It must not appear as a deliberate refusal, nor as disobedience; it must not challenge the norm, but must be presented as a 'mistake,' as an oversight, mishap, error, or one-time weakness that does not call into question the right to expect correct behavior. ... By treating it as a mistake, all traces of personal resentment and aggressiveness are erased. ... The primary purpose of treating it as a mistake is to isolate the disappointing event and strip it of its expressive meaning. Disappointments are, after all,*

---

delicate not so much because of the individual case as because of their repercussions on the generalized structure of expectations. ... Treating it as a mistake, especially the skillful legal handling of the case, distracts from this possibility, cools down the source of the fire, or at least isolates it to itself and to a (preferably only one) culprit." So, deviations are not interpreted as a systemic crisis, but as isolated 'mistakes' in order to ensure the legitimacy and stability of the organisation, but at the price that learning can be blocked.

[72] Hopkins, A. (1995), *Making Safety Work – Getting Management Commitment to Occupational Health and Safety*, St. Leonards: Allen & Unwin. See page 104.

[73] Durkheim, E. (1897), *Le Suicide: Étude de sociologie*, Paris: Ancienne Librairie Germer Bailliere et Cte (Ed. Félix Alcan).

[74] Kühl, S. (2018), *Influencing Organizational Culture – A Very Brief Introduction*, Princeton: Organizational Dialogue Press. On page 26, he writes: *"Even if informal programs, communication channels and decisions on personnel are identified in detail within the framework of a cultural analysis, they are not always related to formal programs, communication channels and personnel decisions. There is a dominant idea that one can understand an organizational-cultural structure without having to grasp in detail how it is shaped by the formal structure, what gaps in the formal structure it fills and where it comes into conflict with the formal structure."*

[75] Power, M. (2004),The risk management of everything, *The Journal of Risk Finance*, Vol. 5, Issue 3, pp. 58 – 65. On page 60, he writes: *"Societies have no option but to organize in the face of risk, and this extends the reach of internal control into every aspect of organization life."* Power's critique is that risk management systems often attempt to bring structure, predictability, and control to areas fundamentally uncertain or resistant to such control.

[76] Kühl, S. (2018), *Influencing Organizational Culture – A Very Brief Introduction*, Princeton: Organizational Dialogue Press. On pages 41-43, he writes that organisational culture is not something that can be changed through catchy metaphors, four-quadrant models, or workshop exercises. These appealing, simple and memorable approaches tend to obscure rather than reveal the actual culture. For Kühl, culture is not a canvas to be repainted with aspirational values or idealised personas, but it's embedded in the habitual, often contradictory routines, silences, and informal practices of daily organisational life. So, culture manifests most tangibly in how safety is managed, measured, and misunderstood, not in posters or mission

statements, but in what is consistently done, tolerated, or left unspoken.

[77] Luhmann, N. (1982), *The Differentiation of Society*, New York: Columbia University Press. On page 236-237, he writes: "*Functional differentiation organizes communication processes around special functions to be fulfilled at the level of society. (...) A functionally differentiated society, as a result, will become, or will have to pretend to be, a society of equals insofar as it is the aggregate set of environments for its functional subsystems*." These statements reflect the change from the shared moral frameworks seen in stratified societies to a society where differentiation by function governs communication and meaning.

[78] It's an OpenAI-remake of an actual Dutch poster about 'safe roadwork'.

[79] Last year, a speed camera was installed near my house. In the last four months of last year alone, 17,981 fines were issued; a national record. In most locations where this type of camera is installed, the number of fines drops significantly over time. Drivers adapt; they drive more slowly. But that does not seem to be the case with the speed camera near me. In the first four months of this year, the same camera was still in the top three of locations where fines were issued in the Netherlands.
In Luhmann's terms, we are dealing with the legal system here, which works via the binary code legal/illegal. It is illegal to drive faster than 50 km/h here. But if our goal is for people to keep to that limit, then the system must take into account what makes such behaviour intuitive. That is the heart of the matter: driving 50 km/h on this road is not self-evident. The road itself communicates something different. The street in question is wide, straight and largely uninterrupted; there is only one side road halfway. The road is used exclusively by motorised traffic; cyclists and pedestrians are physically excluded. The design encourages speed: 70 km/h feels more natural than 50. Importantly, the location is not known for accidents and does not appear in traffic accident statistics. There is no obvious safety problem, only a legal one. That is why the number of fines does not decrease. The infrastructure suggests one behaviour, while the law requires another. And in this tension, it's the road, not the speed limit sign, that wins. - The number of fines were published by: Speerstra, R.J. (2025), 13.839 boetes: flitser in nationale top drie, in: *Heerenveense Courant*, June 19th 2025.

[80] Luhmann, N. (2000), *Organisation und Entscheidung*, Opladen: Westdeutscher Verlag. On page 424, Luhmann

explains that a single decision never equals the organisation/system. It only counts as a decision because it's linked to past and future decisions in the ongoing web of communications. The system is this recursive process, not any one element.

[81] Luhmann, N. (2016), *Zweckbegriff und Systemrationalität*, Frankfurt am Main: Suhrkamp Verlag. On page 321, he writes that complex systems resolve unsolvable problems by transforming them into solvable equivalents, thereby generating "*a proliferation of abstract and specified viewpoints of relative 'insofar as' validity*." These viewpoints concentrate information into decisions that are "*not causally or logically derived from premises but innovatively create order*", distancing themselves from the original problem in the process.

[82] Simon, H.A. (1956), Rational Choice and the Structure of the Environment, in: *Psychological Review*, Vol. 63, Issue 2, pp. 129–138.

[83] March, J.G., Simon, H.A., *Organizations*, Second Edition, Wiley-Blackwell. Extended by Luhmann.

[84] Photo of Ketel Bridge by user European Roads on flickr.com, used with permission.

[85] Wildervanck, C. (2008), Rechterlijke macht, in: *Dagblad van het Noorden*, 3rd of March, 2008.

[86] Luhmann, N., Fuchs, P. (1989), *Reden und schweigen*, Frankfurt am Main: Suhrkamp Verlag.

[87] Baecker, D. (2023), *Form und Formen der Kommunikation*, Frankfurt am Main: Suhrkamp Verlag.

[88] I paraphrase Luhmann here, based on the explanation of his theory by Hans-Georg Moeller, particularly chapter 8 'Individuals and Freedom':

"*The mass media present human beings as 'individuals,' as social agents with certain social characteristics. This presentation cannot do justice to the complexity of human existence—the mass media cannot portray biological or psychic operations. [...] The 'self,' the 'individuality,' and the 'identity' that we deal with today are the effects of the social reality of our time and of its specific coupling with psychic reality*."

This supports my statement that what we identify as 'human' or 'human error' isn't a neutral fact but a constructed distinction within a system. In Luhmann's terms, the observer (i.e. psychological or social system) applies its own logic or code to make sense of behaviour, framing it as error, competence, deviance, etc.

Moeller, H.G. (2006), *Luhmann Explained – From Souls to Systems*, Chicago: Carus.

Luhmann himself wrote: "*The construct of the 'cognitively more or less informed, competent, morally responsible human being' helps the function system of the mass media constantly to irritate itself with regard to its biological and psychic human environment*". This shows that systems don't deal with humans as they are, but with representations or constructs of humans that make sense within the system's logic; just as 'human error' is a label that reflects the system's expectations, not an objective condition. – The quote is on page 74 of:
Luhmann, N. (2000), *The Reality of the Mass Media*, Stanford: Stanford University Press.
[89] Wildervanck, C. (2020), Wat stuurt de bestuurder: Met twee muizen brug bedienen, in: *Dagblad van het Noorden*, Thursday 16th of January ,2020.
[90] Luhmann, N. (2003), *Soziologie des Risikos*, Berlin/New York: Walter de Gruyter. The quote is on page 21.
[91] Luhmann, N. (2017), *Die Kontrolle von Intransparenz*, Frankfurt am Main: Suhrkamp Verlag. On page 47, he writes: „*One could (...) say: an analysis must distinguish between themes and functions of communication. (...) The functions, on the other hand, refer to the contribution to the continuation of communication, that is, to use this term, to the autopoiesis of the system."* This reflects Luhmann's core concept that systems maintain themselves (*autopoiesis*) not by eliminating uncertainty, but by organising meaning through communication.
[92] Reason, J. (1997), *Managing the Risks of Organisational Accidents*, Farnham/Burlington: Ashgate. On page 36, Reason writes: "*If eternal vigilance is the price of liberty, then chronic unease is the price of safety."*
[93] Luhmann, N. (2011), *Organisation und Entscheidung*, 3rd Edition, Wiesbaden: VS Verlag. The text in quotation marks is a synthesis of a paragraph about decision premises. A particularly relevant passage is on page 239: "*Das System kann, wie immer unzulänglich, auf einer höheren Ebene auf das Problem einer simultanen Arbeitsweise reagieren, nämlich darauf, dass gleichzeitig stattfindende Operationen füreinander unerreichbar sind. (...) Nur so können sie Tempo mit Komplexität kombinieren."*
[94] Adapted from Hopkins, A. (2012), *Disastrous Decisions – The Human and Organisational Causes of the Gulf of Mexico Blowout*, Macquarie Park: CCH.
[95] Luhmann, N. (2011), *Organisation und Entscheidung*, 3rd Edition, Wiesbaden: VS Verlag. Again, I took the liberty to paraphrase Luhmann here. The original quote is on page 47: "*Das System kann die eingebaute (...) Unsicherheit nicht in Sicherheit umwandeln. Unsicherheitsabsorption (...) kann nur*

eine Transformation der jeweils aktuellen Form von Unsicherheit sein in Anpassung an wechselnde Zustände der Irritation."

[96] Nassehi says that we need new frameworks that respect distributed intelligence and conflicting logics in society, that avoid reverting to simplistic ideological fixes, and that recognise that modern societies can't be changed top-down, but must be understood through their inner complexity: "*There is no place from which the different dynamics can be steered and coordinated. Not even politics is ultimately capable of that. That's why I speak of a 'distributed intelligence'. (...) Perhaps the role of intellectual observation today must be to question the addressability of society." -*
Poschardt, U. (2015), Was ist heute noch links und was rechts?, in: *Welt.* https://www.welt.de/politik/deutschland/article140991888/Professor-Nassehi-Was-ist-heute-noch-links-und-was-rechts.html

[97] Nassehi, A. (2015), *Die letzte Stunde der Wahrheit, Warum rechts und links keine Alternativen mehr sind und Gesellschaft ganz anders beschrieben werden muss*, Hamburg: Murmann Publishers. The quoted sentences are taken from pages 236 and 237.

[98] This paragraph and the accompanying illustration is adapted from: Rae, D. (2024), False Assurance, *EHS Congress* Berlin 2024, Day 2.

[99] Nassehi, N. (2005), Organizations as decision machines: Niklas Luhmann's theory of organised social systems, in: *The Sociological Review*, Vol. 53, Issue 1. On page 180, he writes: "*On the one hand, this means that a system reduces the possibilities of its future operations. On the other hand, the closing down of possibilities is precisely what enhances the system's ability to develop a special kind of complexity*." So, organisations don't eliminate complexity but selectively reduce it in ways that enable the emergence of new, manageable forms of complexity.

[100] Screenshot from https://eu.greenbaypressgazette.com/story/news/local/2016/01/26/uncertainty-remote-control-bridges/79295066/

[101] Luhmann, N. (2000), *Organisation und Entscheidung*, Opladen: Westdeutscher Verlag. See pages 361-379.

[102] The phrase "Art for Art's Sake" dates back to 19th century France, and embodies the idea that the value of art lies solely in its aesthetic qualities, independent of any moral, social, or practical function. Likewise, Luhmann's systems thinking involves systems with their independent codes, being operationally closed.

---

[103] Mullan, B., Smith, L., Sainsbury, K., Allom, V., Paterson, H., & Lopez, A. L. (2015), Active behaviour change safety interventions in the construction industry: A systematic review, in: *Safety science*, Vol. 79, pp. 139-148.
Spigener, J. Lyon, G., McSween, T. (2022), Behavior-based safety 2022: today's evidence, in: *Journal of Organizational Behavior Management*, Vol. 42, Issue 4, pp. 336-359.
[104] Hollnagel, E. (2014), *Safety-I and Safety-II – The Past and Future of Safety Management*, Farnham/ Burlington: Ashgate. On page 178, Hollnagel writes: "(...) *the way ahead is a combination of the existing practices of Safety-I with the complementary – and to some extent novel – practices of Safety-II* (...)."
[105] See either endnote 17 or 104.
[106] Dekker, S. (2015), *Safety Differently - Human Factors for a New Era*, Second Edition, Boca Raton: CRC Press.
[107] Conklin, T. (2019), *The 5 Principles of Human Performance: A contemporary update of the building blocks of Human Performance for the new view of safety*, Santa Fe: Pre-Accident Investigation Media.
[108] Edwards, B., Baker, A. (2020), *Bob's Guide to Operational Learning: How to Think Like a Human and Organizational Performance (HOP) Coach*, Santa Fe: Pre-Accident Investigation Media.

www.ingramcontent.com/pod-product-compliance
Ingram Content Group UK Ltd.
Pitfield, Milton Keynes, MK11 3LW, UK
UKHW020718041026
15590UKWH00002B/747

9 789083 571706